CW01022719

Good footpath
(sufficiently distinct to be followed in mist)

Intermittent footpath
(difficult to follow in mist)

Route recommended
but no path
(if recommended one way only, arrow indicates direction)

Wall ○○○○○○○○○○○○   **Broken wall** ○ ○ ○ ○ ○ ○ ○ ○ ○ ○ ○ ○ ○ ○

Fence +++++++++++   **Broken fence** ''''''''''''''''''''''''''

Marshy ground   **Trees**

Crags   **Boulders**

Stream or River
(arrow indicates direction of flow)

Waterfall   **Bridge**

Buildings   **Unenclosed road**

Contours (at 100' intervals)   1900
1800
1700

Summit-cairn ▲   **Other** (prominent) **cairns** △

THE
FAR EASTERN
FELLS

A PICTORIAL GUIDE

TO THE

LAKELAND FELLS

50TH ANNIVERSARY EDITION

being an illustrated account
of a study and exploration
of the mountains in the
English Lake District

by

AWainwright

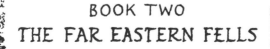

BOOK TWO
THE FAR EASTERN FELLS

Frances Lincoln Limited
4 Torriano Mews
Torriano Avenue
London NW5 2RZ
www.franceslincoln.com

Originally published by Henry Marshall, Kentmere, 1957

First published by Frances Lincoln 2003

50th Anniversary Edition with re-originated artwork
published by Frances Lincoln 2005

Copyright © The Estate of A. Wainwright 1957

All rights reserved. Without limiting the rights under
copyright reserved above, no part of this publication may
be reproduced, stored in or introduced into a retrieval
system, or transmitted, in any form or by any means
(electronic, mechanical, photocopying, or otherwise),
without either prior permission in writing from the
publisher or a licence permitting restricted copying.
In the United Kingdom such licences are issued by
the Copyright Licensing Agency, Saffron House,
6-10 Kirby Street, London EC1N 8TS.

Printed and bound in Thailand

A CIP catalogue record for this book
is available from the British Library.

ISBN 978 0 7112 2455 1

18 17 16 15 14 13 12 11 10

50TH ANNIVERSARY EDITION
PUBLISHED BY
FRANCES LINCOLN, LONDON

THE PICTORIAL GUIDES

Book One: The Eastern Fells, 1955
Book Two: The Far Eastern Fells, 1957
Book Three: The Central Fells, 1958
Book Four: The Southern Fells, 1960
Book Five: The Northern Fells, 1962
Book Six: The North Western Fells, 1964
Book Seven: The Western Fells, 1966

PUBLISHER'S NOTE

This 50th Anniversary edition of the Pictorial Guides to the Lakeland Fells is newly reproduced from the handwritten pages created in the 1950s and 1960s by A. Wainwright. The descriptions of the walks were correct, to the best of the author's knowledge, at the time of first publication and they are reproduced here without amendment. However, footpaths, cairns and other waymarks described here are no longer all as they were fifty years ago and walkers are advised to check with an up-to-date map when planning a walk.

Fellwalking has increased dramatically since the Pictorial Guides were first published. Some popular routes have become eroded, making good footwear and great care all the more necessary for walkers. The vital points about fellwalking, as A. Wainwright himself wrote on many occasions, are to use common sense and to remember to watch where you are putting your feet.

A programme of revision of the Pictorial Guides is under way and revised editions of each of them will be published over the next few years.

BOOK TWO

is dedicated to
the memory of

THE MEN WHO BUILT THE STONE WALLS,

which have endured
the storms of centuries
and remain to this day as monuments to
enterprise, perseverance and hard work

Classification and Definition

Any division of the Lakeland fells into geographical districts must necessarily be arbitrary, just as the location of the outer boundaries of Lakeland must always be a matter of opinion. Any attempt to define internal or external boundaries is certain to invite criticism, and he who takes it upon himself to say where Lakeland starts and finishes, or, for example, where the Central Fells merge into the Southern Fells and *which* fells are the Central Fells and which the Southern and *why* they need be so classified, must not expect his pronouncements to be generally accepted.

Yet for present purposes some plan of classification and definition must be used. County and parochial boundaries are no help, nor is the recently-defined area of the Lakeland National Park, for this book is concerned only with the high ground.

First, the external boundaries. Straight lines linking the extremities of the outlying lakes enclose all the higher fells very conveniently. There are a few fells of lesser height to the north and east, however, that are typically Lakeland in character and cannot properly be omitted : these are brought in, somewhat untidily, by extending the lines in those areas. Thus :

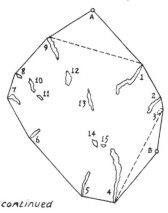

1 : *Ullswater*
2 : *Hawes Water*
3 : proposed *Swindale Res.*
4 : *Windermere*
5 : *Coniston Water*
6 : *Wast Water*
7 : *Ennerdale Water*
8 : *Loweswater*
9 : *Bassenthwaite Lake*
10 : *Crummock Water*
11 : *Buttermere*
12 : *Derwent Water*
13 : *Thirlmere*
14 : *Grasmere*
15 : *Rydal Water*
A : *Caldbeck*
B : *Longsleddale* (church)

continued

Classification and Definition
continued

The complete Guide is planned to include all the fells in the area enclosed by the straight lines of the diagram. This is an undertaking quite beyond the compass of a single volume, and it is necessary, therefore, to divide the area into convenient sections, making the fullest use of natural boundaries (lakes, valleys and low passes) so that each district is, as far as possible, self-contained and independent of the rest.

This division gives seven areas, each with a well-defined group of fells, and each will be the subject of a separate volume

1 : The Eastern Fells
2 : The Far Eastern Fells
3 : The Central Fells
4 : The Southern Fells
5 : The Northern Fells
6 : The North-western Fells
7 : The Western Fells

Notes on the Illustrations

THE MAPS.................. Many excellent books have been written about Lakeland, but the best literature of all for the walker is that published by the Director General of Ordnance Survey, the 1" map for companionship and guidance on expeditions, the 2½" map for exploration both on the fells and by the fireside. These admirable maps are remarkably accurate topographically but there is a crying need for a revision of the paths on the hills: several walkers' tracks that have come into use during the past few decades, some of them now broad highways, are not shown at all; other paths still shown on the maps have fallen into neglect and can no longer be traced on the ground.

The popular Bartholomew 1" map is a beautiful picture, fit for a frame, but this too is unreliable for paths; indeed here the defect is much more serious, for routes are indicated where no paths ever existed, nor ever could — the cartographer has preferred to take precipices in his stride rather than deflect his graceful curves over easy ground.

Hence the justification for the maps in this book: they have the one merit (of importance to walkers) of being dependable as regards delineation of *paths*. They are intended as supplements to the Ordnance Survey maps, certainly not as substitutes.

THE VIEWS............... Various devices have been used to illustrate the views from the summits of the fells. The full panorama in the form of an outline drawing is most satisfactory generally, and this method has been adopted for the main viewpoints.

THE DIAGRAMS OF ASCENTS.................... The routes of ascent of the higher fells are depicted by diagrams that do not pretend to strict accuracy: they are neither plans nor elevations; in fact there is deliberate distortion in order to show detail clearly: usually they are represented as viewed from imaginary 'space-stations.' But it is hoped they will be useful and interesting.

THE DRAWINGS....... The drawings at least are honest attempts to reproduce what the eye sees: they illustrate features of interest and also serve the dual purpose of breaking up the text and balancing the layout of the pages, and of filling up awkward blank spaces, like this:

Thirlmere

THE
FAR EASTERN FELLS

The Far Eastern Fells rise to the east of Kirkstone Pass and the Patterdale valley, which together form a natural western boundary to the group. To north and south these fells run down to low country, and it is on the east side that difficulty arises in fixing a demarcation line, for here high ground continues, to merge ultimately into the Pennines. Nevertheless, it is possible to adopt a satisfactory boundary, not so much by a selection of obvious natural features as by observation of the characteristics of the fells in this area. Lakeland's fells have a charm that is unique: they are romantic in atmosphere, dramatic in appearance, colourful, craggy, with swift-running sparkling streams and tumbled lichened boulders — and the walker along this eastern fringe constantly finds himself passing from the exciting beauty that is typically Lakeland to the quieter and more sombre attractiveness that is typically Pennine. Broadly, this 'æsthetic' boundary runs along the eastern watersheds of Longsleddale, Mosedale and Swindale.

The group has a main spine running through it, due north and south, that keeps consistently above 2000' over a distance of eight miles and culminates midway in the greatest of these fells, High Street. From this central point there is a general decline in altitude towards the boundaries of the group in all directions but it is not to be inferred that all ridges radiate from High Street: on the contrary, it is the pivot of a complicated system of parallel and lateral ridges separated by deep valleys that contributes greatly to the attractiveness of these fells east of Kirkstone.

The relative inaccessibility of many of the heights (due to a decided lack of tourist accommodation in the valleys) can be the only reason why they remain lonely and unfrequented by visitors, for in the high quality of the scenery and the excellence of the walks they rank with the best. In one respect, indeed, they are supreme, for their extensive and uplifting views across to the distant Pennines are a delight not to be found elsewhere in the district. Solitary walkers will enjoy the area immensely, but they must tread circumspectly and avoid accident. Mountain-camps and bivouacs offer the best means of exploration; for the walker who prefers a bed, Mardale Head used to be the best centre but now has no hospitality nearer than the Haweswater Hotel (which is badly sited for travellers on foot) and the Patterdale valley is most convenient as a base. The area will be appreciated best, however, if occasional nights can be arranged at Howtown, Haweswater, Kentmere and Troutbeck.

THE FAR EASTERN FELLS

Natural Boundaries

MILES

POOLEY BRIDGE
ASKHAM

River Lowther

ULLSWATER

Goldrill Beck

Kirkstone Pass

Stock Gill

AMBLESIDE

HAWESWATER

Swindale Beck

Little Mosedale Beck

LONG SLEDDALE

KENTMERE

TROUTBECK

N

ALTITUDE OF FELLS
  below 2000'
  2000'–2500'
  over 2500'

Identification numbers are in descending order of altitude: key on opposite page

THE FAR EASTERN FELLS

in the order of
their appearance
in this book

Each fell is the subject
of a separate chapter

Angletarn Pikes

Howtown •

▲ PLACE FELL

• Patterdale

▲ ANGLETARN
PIKES

• Hartsop

HIGH STREET ▲

MILES
0 1 2 3 4

from Brothers Water

NATURAL FEATURES

The distinctive double summit of Angletarn Pikes is a familiar feature high above the Patterdale valley: the two sharp peaks arrest attention from a distance and are no less imposing on close acquaintance, being attainable only by rock-scrambling, easy or difficult according to choice of route. The western flank of the fell drops steeply in slopes of bracken to the pleasant strath of the Goldrill Beck; on this side Dubhow Crag and Fall Crag are prominent. More precipitous is the eastern face overlooking the quiet deer sanctuary of Bannerdale, where the great bastion of Heck Crag is a formidable object rarely seen by walkers. The fell is a part of a broad curving ridge that comes down from the High Street watershed and continues to Boardale Hause, beyond which Place Fell terminates it abruptly.

The crowning glory of the Pikes, however, is the tarn from which they are named, cradled in a hollow just below the summit. Its indented shore and islets are features unusual in mountain tarns, and it has for long, and deservedly, been a special attraction for visitors to Patterdale. The charms of Angle Tarn, at all seasons of the year, are manifold: in scenic values it ranks amongst the best of Lakeland tarns.

1 : The summit
2 : The summit of Brock Crags
3 : Boardale Hause
4 : Ridge continuing to Beda Fell
5 : Ridge continuing to Rest Dodd
6 : Heck Crag
7 : Fall Crag
8 : Dubhow Crag
9 : Bannerdale
10 : Angle Tarn
11 : Dubhow Beck
12 : Angletarn Beck
13 : Goldrill Beck
14 : Brothers Water
15 : Hayeswater Gill

looking
north

Red Screes and
Brothers Water
from the top of
Dubhow Beck

Heck Crag
from the
Patterdale-
Martindale path

MAP

ONE MILE

ASCENT FROM PATTERDALE
1400 feet of ascent : 1¾ miles
Note that this is the initial part of the route to High Street

ANGLETARN PIKES

←BEDA FELL

1800
1700

HIGH STREET→

Angle Tarn

The variation by Freeze Beck is unfrequented and the path is not clear at its start (by a cairn)

1600

1500

Dubhow Beck

Beautiful view from the path above Dubhow Beck

Freeze Beck

grass

MARTINDALE ---→

1500

ravine

1400

Dubhow Crag

Rake Crag

Boardale Hause

1300

sheepfold

BOARDALE ←---

fold

PLACE FELL ←---

post

sheepfold

Recent pipelaying operations have obscured temporarily some paths on Boardale Hause

line of aqueduct

HARTSOP 1½ →

The two paths rising across the fellside to Boardale Hause run closely parallel, but it is not a matter of indifference which is taken, as is often thought. Each has its own objectives, the higher (left) leading to Boardale or Place Fell, the lower (right) to Martindale or Angle Tarn.

1000

900

800

Stonebarrow Gill

700

bracken

ROAD to HARTSOP 2 and KIRKSTONE PASS

Gain access to the paths through a gate that bears the inspiring notice 'TO THE FELL'

seat x

larch plantation

LANE to CROOKABECK ½ and HARTSOP 2

600

LAKESIDE PATH to SANDWICH ←---

LANE to SIDE FARM

Goldrill Bridge

White Lion Hotel

looking south-east

Patterdale   Patterdale Hotel

This delightful walk should be in the itinerary of all who stay at Patterdale; the climb is pleasant and the views excellent. Combined with a detour to Angle Tarn, it is an easy half-day's excursion.

ASCENT FROM MARTINDALE
1300 feet of ascent : 3½ miles from Martindale Old Church

ANGLETARN PIKES

looking west

Angle Tarn · Buck Crag · Heck Crag · Heck Cove · Broad Crags · ruins · Bedafell Knott · BEDA FELL

In faded letters, with Victorian courtesy, the old notice board requests VISITORS AND TOURISTS not to trespass in the deer forest.

notice board · boulder · gate · gate · gate · fold · ruin · Bannerdale Beck · Dalehead

Dalehead farmhouse is interesting architecturally

ROAD TO MARTINDALE CHURCH 1½

Two routes are illustrated; both are good.

The valley route, by the wall, is an example of a beautiful and interesting footway falling from favour simply because few now know of it. It ascends the secluded and unfrequented valley of Bannerdale, passes below Heck Crag by a sporting path on steep scree and crosses a low saddle to Angle Tarn, which comes into view suddenly and dramatically: the highlight of the walk. An easy climb (right) leads to the top.

The more direct way makes use of the path to Patterdale, but turns left when the ridge is gained and keeps to the Bannerdale edge until the summit is close on the right.

If the return is to be made to Martindale, use the valley route for the ascent (because of the sudden revelation of Angle Tarn, a surprise worth planning) and the ridge route for descent.

THE SUMMIT

The north (main) summit

Angle Tarn from the south summit

Twin upthrusts of rock, 200 yards apart, give individuality to this unusual summit; the northerly is the higher. Otherwise the top is generally grassy, with an extensive peat bog in a depression.

DESCENTS : Routes of ascent may be reversed. (Note that, to find the Bannerdale valley-path, it is necessary first to descend to Angle Tarn and there cross the low saddle on the left at a boulder opposite the peninsula). *In mist*, there is comfort in knowing that the path for Patterdale is only 100 yards distant down the west slope.

THE VIEW

Principal Fells

Although the view is largely confined by surrounding heights to a five-mile radius it is full of interest. The abrupt summit gives splendid depth and fall to the prospect south-west, where there is a beautiful picture of Brothers Water and Kirkstonefoot. Deepdale, directly below, is especially well seen.

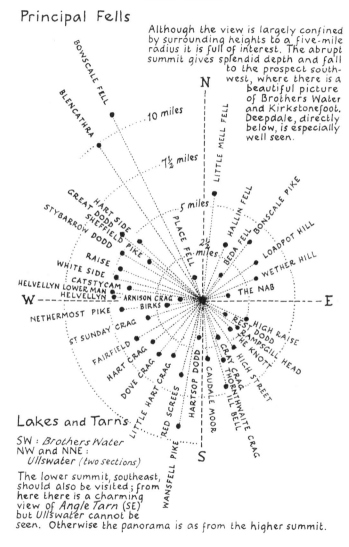

Lakes and Tarns

SW: *Brothers Water*
NW and NNE:
   Ullswater (two sections)

The lower summit, southeast, should also be visited; from here there is a charming view of *Angle Tarn* (SE) but *Ullswater* cannot be seen. Otherwise the panorama is as from the higher summit.

RIDGE ROUTES

To BEDA FELL, 1664' : 2 miles
NE, then N and NE   *300 feet*
Main depression at 1450'   *of ascent*
and several minor depressions

An easy walk, the latter part being dull.
Aim for the high knoll north-east, where
an intermittent path leads down a
narrowing shoulder (good views of
Bannerdale and Heck Crag here).
The Patterdale-Martindale path
is crossed as it tops the ridge.
Beyond, the walk becomes
uninteresting. Beda Fell is
dangerous in mist, having
precipitous crags on the
eastern flank, and the
ridge is ill-defined
beyond the summit.

BEDA FELL
▲ (BEDA HEAD)

The
Patterdale-
Martindale
path is an easy
way of escape
in bad weather, but
must be watched
for carefully;
it is indistinct
as it crosses the ridge.

ONE MILE

N

PATTERDALE

MARTINDALE

Bedafell Knott ▲

ruin

Broad Crags

Heck Cove

Heck Crag

ANGLETARN PIKES ▲

To REST DODD, 2278'
1¾ miles : SE, then E
Depression at 1600'.
700 feet of ascent.
An easy climb;
route confusing in mist.
Descend to Angle Tarn and
there join the path for High
Street, leaving it at Satura
Crag in favour of a shoulder
that rises to the final dome
*but in mist keep to the fence
and wall from Satura Crag.*

ANGLETARN PIKES

ONE MILE

N

Angle Tarn

Buck Crag

Bannerdale

Satura Crag

gate

REST DODD ▲

BROCK CRAGS

gate

broken fence

From the cairn on Satura Crag
(only 25 yards from the path)
there is a splendid view of
Bannerdale, a view often
missed by walkers
along this route.

- • Pooley Bridge
- Askham

- ▲ ARTHUR'S PIKE
- • Howtown
- ▲ LOADPOT HILL

MILES
0 1 2 3 4

from the Howtown road

NATURAL FEATURES

Arthur's Pike is the northerly termination of the long High Street range, and, like the northerly termination of the parallel Helvellyn range, it contrasts with the usual Lakeland fell-structure by exhibiting its crags to the afternoon sun; the northern and eastern slopes, which are commonly roughest, are without rock. The steep flank falling to Ullswater has several faces of crag below the summit-rim, and, especially around the vicinity of Swarthbeck Gill, which forms the southern boundary of the fell, acres of tumbled boulders testify to the roughness of the impending cliffs and the power of the beck in flood. Above the crags, there is little to excite, and the summit merges without much change in elevation into the broad expanses of Loadpot Hill. The gradual northern slope is clothed with heather.

MAP

ONE MILE

Note that the scale of this map is smaller than that commonly used in this book (in order to include the full Howtown route)

The Howtown path accompanies the Hayeswater Aqueduct

Ullswater, from the Howtown path

ASCENTS

Arthur's Pike looks particularly forbidding from the Howtown path, by which it is usually climbed, and the timid walker who doubts the wisdom of proceeding will be reassured to discover that the ascent is not only not intimidating but surprisingly easy and everywhere pleasant, *if the route shown on the map is followed.* The obvious and direct alternative by the Swarthbeck ravine is anything but obvious and direct when attempted, and nervous pedestrians should keep away from it.

For the approaches from Askham, Helton and Pooley Bridge, the chapter on Loadpot Hill should be consulted.

THE SUMMIT

Above the edge of the steep Ullswater flank, grassy undulations culminate in a conical knoll crowned by a large cairn; nearby is a shelter (from wind) in a short wall. There are no paths on the top, but an indefinite cairned track skirts the precipice, on the brink of which is a collapsed beacon; and on the eastern side is a fairly good path that goes nowhere in particular in either direction and is of little use to the walker. The beacon cannot be seen from the summit-cairn; it stands 250 yards distant in the direction of Blencathra.

THE VIEW

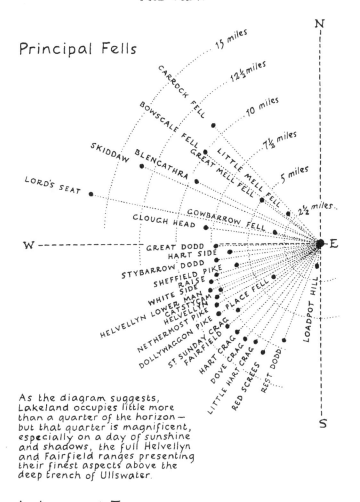

Principal Fells

As the diagram suggests, Lakeland occupies little more than a quarter of the horizon — but that quarter is magnificent, especially on a day of sunshine and shadows, the full Helvellyn and Fairfield ranges presenting their finest aspects above the deep trench of Ullswater.

Lakes and Tarns

W to N: *Ullswater (two sections: middle and lower reaches)*
Ullswater is better seen from the beacon: an impressive sight.

RIDGE ROUTES

To LOADPOT HILL, 2201': 2¼ miles
S, then SSW, SSE and finally N

Minor depressions : 500 feet of ascent
A dull, easy walk, not recommended in mist

Aim for the low hill due south, crossing a good path on the way, and join there the old High Street, which is now indistinct in places and at its best only a series of ruts in the grass, often marshy. When the dome of Loadpot Hill is reached, the path becomes an ascending groove, easy to follow; it turns away downhill just short of the ruins of Lowther House, where turn north to the summit cairn, which encloses a boundary stone. *This is not a walk for a wet day, and the whole of this moorland is a nightmare in mist.*

To BONSCALE PIKE, 1718'
1 mile : S. then SSW and NW
Depression at 1575'
150 feet of ascent

A simple walk which should not be attempted in mist.

Join the good path running east of the summit and follow it south to a sheepfold in the depression between the two Pikes. Cross the beck and slant over grassy slopes to the right. *Swarthbeck Gill is dangerous below the fold.*

Ullswater, from the beacon

Swarthbeck Gill

Swarthbeck Gill, if it were but more accessible, would be one of the showplaces of the district. Here, between towering rockwalls, are beautiful cataracts, but, alas, they are out of the reach of the average explorer. The ferny, tree-clad lower gorge, however, may (and should) be visited. The prudent venture no further!

Beda Fell

1664'

summit named Beda Head

from Hallin Fell

Beda Fell is the long north-east ridge of Angletarn Pikes, narrowing as it descends; but midway it asserts itself, broadens considerably and rises to a definite summit, Beda Head, which is the geographical centre of the quiet, enchanting, exquisitely beautiful area known affectionately as "Martind'l." Beyond this top the descent continues over the rocky spine of Winter Crag to valley-level at Sandwick on Ullswater. The fell, although mainly grassy, with bracken, has a most impressive east face, broken into three great tiers of crag. It is bounded by deep valleys, Boardale, Bannerdale and Howe Grain, whose combined waters meet at its northern tip.

MAP

Bridge in Boardale

ONE MILE

N

Boardale

Boardalehead
(*Bore*dalehead
on Bartholomews
and the 2½"
Ordnance
maps)

Boardale Beck

Boardale Beck

SANDWICK
SANDWICK (path)

Howegrain Beck

HOWTOWN (road)

HOWTOWN (road)

church

Howegrain Beck

Howe Grain (Martindale)

Winter Crag

Thrang Crag

Raven Crag

Allen Crag

Low Brock Crags

1664
BEDA FELL
(BEDA HEAD)

Brock Crag

Dalehead

gate

gate

gate

moraine

Bedafell Knott

ruin

Red Scar

Broad Crags

Heck Cove

Freeze Beck

notice board

Bannerdale Beck

Bannerdale

continuation PLACE FELL 3

continuation ANGLETARN PIKES 4

FARMS
INDICATED
BY NUMBERS
1: Nettleslack
  (derelict)
2: Garth Head
3: Wintercrag
4: Thrangcrag
5: Henhow (ruin)

ASCENTS FROM MARTINDALE AND BOARDALE
1100 feet of ascent : 1¾ miles

The fell is best climbed along its north ridge, over the serrated crest of Winter Crag. The ridge may be gained directly at its extremity from the unenclosed road curving round its tip (in high summer, this route involves a tussle with bracken) or by the short paths from Wintercrag Farm and Garth Head. The ridge of Winter Crag is very enjoyable, but the final slope is dreary, although it may be improved by keeping well to the left to look down the crags into Martindale.

DESCENTS : Use the routes of ascent for returning, unless an extension of the walk is desired, in which case the ridge may be continued south-west as far as the Patterdale-Martindale path and a descent made along it.

In mist, exceeding care is necessary to avoid getting entangled among the crags on the east (Martindale) flank, Allen Crag especially being dangerous. In such conditions, it is advisable to descend from the lower cairn, 150 yards northwest, keeping always to the ridge

THE SUMMIT

The highest point, Beda Head, is an uninteresting mound set upon undulating grassy slopes. Infinitely more exciting and attractive is the rocky top of Winter Crag along the ridge.

THE VIEW

Principal Fells

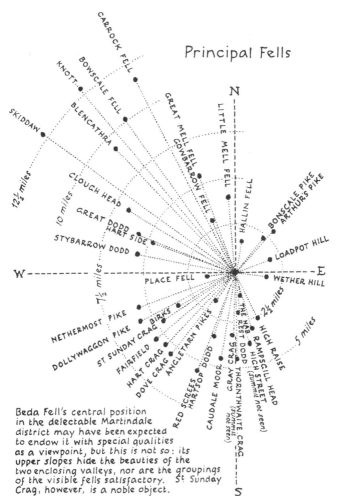

Beda Fell's central position in the delectable Martindale district may have been expected to endow it with special qualities as a viewpoint, but this is not so: its upper slopes hide the beauties of the two enclosing valleys, nor are the groupings of the visible fells satisfactory. St Sunday Crag, however, is a noble object.

Lakes and Tarns

N to NE: *Ullswater* (two sections, divided by *Hallin Fell*)

RIDGE ROUTE

To ANGLETARN PIKES, 1857'
2 miles : SW, then S and SW
*Main depression at 1450'
and several minor depressions*

An easy walk on grass, increasing in interest
Follow the narrowing ridge southwest;
occasional traces of a path may be
found. The first craggy rise, with a
cairn, is Bedafell Knott; beyond it
the main Patterdale-Martindale
path is crossed as it tops the ridge.
From the cairn above Broad Crags
a slight track skirts the eastern
edge of the ridge (striking
view of Heck Crag here).
The final rise ahead
may be avoided on the
right, aiming directly
for the main Pike
now in sight across
a depression.

*In mist, the latter
part of this route
(beyond the cross-path)
is not recommended*

BEDA FELL
(BEDA HEAD)

1600
1500
1400
1300

MARTINDALE

N

ONE MILE

Bedafell Knott
× ruin

Broad Crags

Heck Cove

Heck Crag

PATTERDALE
1500
1600
1700
1800

ANGLETARN PIKES
1800

1600

The Patterdale-Martindale
path is indistinct as it crosses
the ridge. This is the sort of
place a good fell-walker will
memorise so that he may
afterwards recognise it in
misty or snowy conditions!

The ridge south from the cairn
above Broad Crags; on the right
the main Angletarn Pike.

Beda Fell
from
Martindale Old Church

Bonscale Pike

1718'

sometimes referred to as
Swarth Fell

named Toughmoss Pike
on Bartholomew's map

from Hallin Fell

- Pooley Bridge

▲ ARTHUR'S PIKE
▲ BONSCALE PIKE
Howtown
♠ LOADPOT HILL

MILES
0 1 2 3 4

NATURAL FEATURES

Rising steeply behind the little hamlet of Howtown is a broad buttress of the High Street range, Swarth Fell, the turretted and castellated rim of which has the appearance, when seen from Ullswater far below, of the ruined battlements of a castle wall: this aspect is sufficiently arresting to earn for the rocky facade and the summit above it the separate and distinctive name of Bonscale Pike. This escarpment, however, is a sham, for it defends nothing other than a dreary plateau of grass; and indeed there is little else of interest on the fell — excepting Swarthbeck Gill, its northern boundary, which abounds in interest but is out of bounds for the walker because of its obvious dangers. Bonscale Pike presents a bold front, that overlooking the lake, but on all other sides it loses its identity in the high mass of land supporting the great dome of Loadpot Hill.

MAP

ONE MILE

ASCENT FROM HOWTOWN
1200 feet of ascent : 1¼ miles

ARTHUR'S PIKE ← — — · sheepfold 1700 · LOADPOT HILL · LOADPOT HILL · LOADPOT HILL

BONSCALE PIKE

Clumsy pedestrians should keep away from Swarthbeck Gill, which is dangerous.

Swarthbeck Gill

grass

natural groove

groove · 1700

groove · 1600

groove · 1500

1400 · cairn on a boulder · scree · 1400

1300

good path

1200
1100
1000 · bracken

ARTHUR'S PIKE and MOOR DIVOCK

bracken · 900

bracken · 800

seat · 700 · gate · Mellguards

FUSEDALE

gate

Howtown Hotel

Two routes are recommended, and they are indicated on the diagram by arrows: preferably, the route across the breast should be used for ascent and that south along the top for descent.

looking east·south·east

The work of a craftsman
Bonscale Tower

The effort of amateurs
The higher pillar

THE SUMMIT

Neither of the two stone pillars seen so prominently against the skyline from below marks the highest point, this being a grassy hummock between and behind them, with a small cairn. It is an unsatisfactory summit because higher ground rises immediately beyond on the long undulating slope to Loadpot Hill; it does, however, indicate an excellent viewpoint, and also defines the limit of interest, which is centred in the broken wall of crag immediately below. Bonscale Pike, in fact, gives a display of rock-scenery that would improve many a bigger fell. And the men who selected the sites for the two pillars surely had a good appreciation of drama!

DESCENTS: The alternative route of ascent should be used as a way down in order to get the full benefit of the views, but in any case the length of the summit should be traversed.

In mist, a stranger may well feel cause for anxiety. The lower (in altitude), i.e. the northerly, of the two pillars should be rounded above it, by an ample margin, to reach the path below the crags, after which the slope may safely be descended anywhere if the path is lost. Note that the two pillars both stand on the brink of crags. Resist any temptation to slant down to the stream — Swarthbeck Gill is highly dangerous.

Plan of the summit

100 yards

THE VIEW

Principal Fells

The distant fell peeping over the skyline, right of Arthur's Pike, is Cross Fell the highest of the Pennines

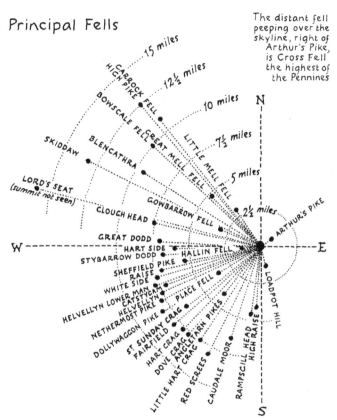

15 miles
12½ miles
10 miles
7½ miles
5 miles
2½ miles

CARROCK FELL
HIGH PIKE
BOWSCALE FELL
GREAT MELL FELL
LITTLE MELL FELL
SKIDDAW
BLENCATHRA
LORD'S SEAT
(summit not seen)
CLOUGH HEAD
GOWBARROW FELL
ARTHUR'S PIKE

N
E
W
S

GREAT DODD
HART SIDE
HALLIN FELL
STYBARROW DODD
SHEFFIELD PIKE
RAISE
WHITE SIDE
HELVELLYN LOWER MAN
CATSTYCAM
HELVELLYN
NETHERMOST PIKE
PLACE FELL
DOLLYWAGGON PIKE
ST SUNDAY CRAG
FAIRFIELD
HART CRAG
DOVE CRAG
ANGLETARN PIKES
LITTLE HART CRAG
RED SCREES
CAUDALE MOOR
RAMPSGILL HEAD
HIGH RAISE
LOADPOT HILL

The prospect of the Helvellyn and Fairfield ranges, although crowded into a quarter-circle, is excellent, and the more distant northern fells are nicely grouped. In other directions there is little to be seen but the nearby dreary slopes falling from Loadpot Hill. The pillars are better viewpoints.

Lakes and Tarns
W to N: Ullswater (middle and lower reaches) — better seen from either of the two pillars

RIDGE ROUTES

To ARTHUR'S PIKE, 1747': 1 mile
SE, then NNE and N
Depression at 1575'
200 feet of ascent
A simple walk, needing care in mist
Slant down a grass slope *south-east*
to the beck, crossing it above a
sheepfold and doubling back
along the opposite slope, where
a fair path will be joined : this
path skirts the summit, and
must be left to visit the cairn.
Short cuts across Swarthbeck Gill,
especially in mist, are dangerous.

To LOADPOT HILL, 2201': 1½ miles
S, then SSE and finally N
Minor depressions
550 feet of ascent
An easy walk, not recommended in mist
Cross the undulating plateau
southwards until the ground
steepens into the vast dome
of Loadpot Hill. A short climb
brings the old High Street (a
grassy groove) underfoot : it
leads to the ruins of Lowther
House, where turn north to
the handsome cairn.

ONE MILE

Ullswater:
the middle reach

Branstree

2333'

(a corruption of Brant Street)
The summit is not named
on Ordnance Survey maps

*from the south-east
ridge of
High Raise*

Haweswater Hotel
●
● Swindale Head

Mardale ▲ SELSIDE PIKE
Head ●

▲ BRANSTREE

▲ HARTER FELL

MILES

0   1   2   3   4

NATURAL FEATURES

Branstree occupies a fine position at the head of three valleys, Mardale, Swindale and Longsleddale, and a fourth, Mosedale, runs along its southern base. This geographical attribute aside, the fell is dreary, and must disappoint all who climb it, for a good deal of perambulation is necessary across the flat and featureless top before these valleys can be brought sufficiently into view for full appreciation. All is grass, although there is a slight boulder-slope below Artlecrag Pike (extravagantly hachured as a crag on most maps), and a remarkable dry gully, the result of a landslide, cleaves the fellside on the Mardale flank from top to bottom. Eastwards there are some subsidiary summits, and a line of crags overlooking Swindale; there is an odd little hanging valley, and noble hidden waterfalls on this side. The Mosedale flank has been extensively quarried. Mosedale Beck is the principal stream: it runs into Swindale Beck, on which Manchester Corporation have covetous eyes.

*High Street
from the north ridge*

MAP

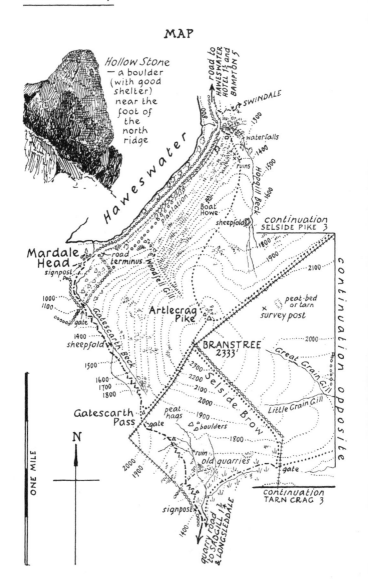

Hollow Stone — a boulder (with good shelter) near the foot of the north ridge

road to HAWESWATER HOTEL 1¼ and BAMPTON 5

SWINDALE

waterfalls

Hopgill Beck

ruins

Haweswater

plantation

Boat Howe

sheepfold

continuation SELSIDE PIKE 3

Mardale Head

signpost

road terminus

Woodall Gill

continuation opposite

peat-bed or tarn

survey post

Artlecrag Pike

gate

sheepfold

BRANSTREE 2333

Great Grain Gill

Gatescarth Beck

Selside Brow

Little Grain Gill

2000

Gatescarth Pass

peat hags

boulders

gate

ruin

old quarries

gate

continuation TARN CRAG 3

signpost

quarry road to SADGILL 1¼ & LONGSLEDDALE

ONE MILE

N

The survey post

MAP

SWINDALE HEAD and road to ROSGILL 4

Swindale

Dodd Bottom

waterfalls

waterfalls

900
1000
1100
1200
1300
1400

Nabs Moor

Mosedale Beck

N

ONE MILE

continuation SELSIDE PIKE 4

2000
1900

Hobgrumble Gill

Howes

1800
1700
1600
1500
1400

gate

fold

fold

ruin

plank bridge

SHAP 6 (distinct path)

Mosedale Quarry (disused)

gates

gate

1800

Great Grain Gill

falls

Mosedale Cottage

Mosedale Beck

Mosedale

1500

continuation opposite

The cairn on Artlecrag Pike

ASCENT FROM MARDALE
1500 feet of ascent : 1½ miles from the road

BRANSTREE

survey post

SELSIDE PIKE ←

grass

Artlecrag Pike

Gatescarth Pass

gate

A series of fine waterfalls adds interest to the steep start.

sheepfold grass ridge

Hopgill Beck

north ridge

Woodfell Gill

scree

Gatescarth Beck

sheepfold

groove

Boat Howe

ruins

boulders bracken

x signpost

NAN BIELD PASS

road terminus

Haweswater

Mardale Head

road to HAWESWATER HOTEL 1½

A wicket gate at the bridge gives access to the fell. Keep out of the gorge.

The ruined walls and neglected paths running down into the water remain mute witnesses to the tragedy of Mardale.

looking south-east

The merit of the ascent by the north ridge lies in its intimate views of Mardale Head and Harter Fell, the climbing itself being dull after a promising start. The Gatescarth route is better used for the return.

ASCENT FROM LONGSLEDDALE

Gatescarth Pass

gate

BRANSTREE

peat hags

boulders

Selside Brow

old quarry

signpost

sheepfold

old quarry

gate

MOSEDALE

looking north

SADGILL 2

1750 feet of ascent
3½ miles from Sadgill

Beware loose wire in the grass alongside the fence above Gatescarth Pass

By any standards, and by any route, the climbing on this flank is completely uninteresting.

THE SUMMIT

highest point

The 'official' watershed is about eighty yards north of the end of the wall; this is the highest point (2333')

The summit is grassy and flat-topped. There is no cairn on the highest point, which is situated near the junction of a well-built wall and the wire fence that traverses the fell. A better place for a halt is the fine cairn on Artlecrag Pike nearby, north-east; here also is some rock to relieve the drab surroundings.

DESCENTS: The quickest way off, and the safest in bad weather, is by the fence to Gatescarth Pass (beware loose wire in the grass, and watch for the gate that indicates the path for Longsleddale, left, and Mardale, right). The most attractive descent is that by the north ridge for Mardale, with good views of Haweswater.

RIDGE ROUTE

To TARN CRAG, 2176'
1¼ miles : SE, then S
Depression at 1650'
550 feet of ascent
Easy gradients ; a dull walk

Features of interest are lacking on this moorland trudge. Care is needed on Tarn Crag in mist.

highest point ✕ BRANSTREE

N

Selside Brow

2300
2200
2100
2000
1900

ONE MILE

grass
1800
1700

LONGSLEDDALE ← gate → SWINDALE and SHAP

peat hags
1700
1800
1900
2000
2100

traces of cart track

grass

TARN CRAG ▲ ✕ survey post

Harter Crag from the slopes of Branstree

RIDGE ROUTES

To HARTER FELL, 2539': 2 miles: SW then NW and SW
Depression at 1875' (Gatescarth Pass): 700 feet of ascent
    An easy walk on grass.   Safe in mist, with care

Loose wire alongside the fence going down to Gatescarth Pass is a snare for the unsuspecting walker, especially he who travels at speed. When the fence turns, continue along the line marked by the fragmentary remains of an old fence, which can be traced to the summit. In mist, this line must be followed carefully.

To SELSIDE PIKE, 2142': 1½ miles: NE
Two shallow depressions: 200 feet of ascent
    An easy walk on grass, safe in mist

Visit the fine cairn on Artlecrag Pike, then cross the fence to the old survey post and traverse the knoll beyond (no cairn; view of Helvellyn here). *In mist, keep to the fence linking the two summits.*

The survey post was built by Manchester Corporation during the construction of the Haweswater Aqueduct. It does not stand on the crest of the depression, as might have been expected, but slightly below it; the top of the post, however, overtops the crest and the next survey post, on Tarn Crag, is visible from it (south).

THE VIEW

Principal Fells

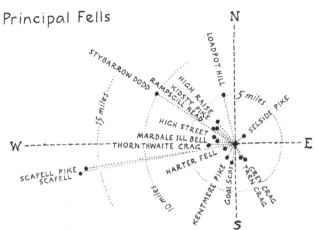

Lakes and Tarns

Branstree is one of the very few Lakeland fells that have no view of lakes or tarns from the highest point, but Haweswater is brought into view by walking a few paces north. The long strip of water in the distance southwards is the Kent estuary.

Despite Branstree's good geographical position, little is seen of Lakeland: the lofty skyline of the Mardale heights admits only two small vistas of distant fells. Compensation is found, however, in the wide prospect of the Pennines. An interesting feature is the glimpse of the Scafells with Mickledore — note that, of this group, only the Pike is in view from the wall end.

Mosedale Cottage — occasionally occupied by shepherds

Brock Crags

1842'

from Goldrill Beck

Patterdale

ANGLE TARN
▲ PIKES

BROCK ▲ CRAGS
• Hartsop

HIGH STREET ▲

MILES

0   1   2   3   4

The unspoilt village of Low Hartsop
has great charm and its environment
is one of quiet loveliness, much of it
contributed by the hanging woods of
the steep fell that rises immediately
behind. This fell, Brock Crags, is an
offshoot of a ridge coming down to
Ullswater from the main High Street
watershed, and overlooks a meeting
of many valleys: a feature in the
view from the rocky top. Its slopes
carry the Hayeswater aqueduct, and
recent pipelaying operations there
have left an ugly scar along its fair
breast. Nature is a great healer:
it cannot heal too swiftly here.

MAP

PATH TO PATTERDALE 1¾

ROAD TO PATTERDALE 1¾

Continuation ANGLETARN PIKES 4

PATTERDALE 2

PATH TO PATTERDALE 1¼

Angletarn Beck

Fall Crag

falls

Cal Crag

Calf Close

Lingy Crag

N

BROCK CRAGS
1842 ▲

1800

1600
1500
1400
1300

gate

gate

REST DODD

aqueduct

Low Hartsop

Goldrill Beck

Brothers Water

ROAD TO KIRKSTONE PASS

filter house

Hayeswater Gill

HAYESWATER 1

old shaft

ONE MILE

ASCENT FROM HARTSOP
1300 feet of ascent : 1 mile

The exit from Hartsop is not clear. Either (a) start along a lane opposite a turning-space for cars near the end of the village, soon bearing right along a grass path between walls (ignore the road going left) and then uphill across an enclosure to the pipeline. Or (b) follow the cart track up the valley to the filter-house, turning back along the pipeline at a higher level. Above the pipeline, find

BROCK CRAGS

shelter under crag

grooved path

Pipeline

Hayeswater Aqueduct

Pipeline

ruin

pastures

cart-track

Hayeswater Gill

gate

Hartsop

filter house

1800
1700
1600
1500
1400
1300
1200
1000
900
800

looking north

a grooved path ascending right through a gap in an old wall: it becomes indistinct at 1600, the summit then being over easy slopes to the left. Or follow the old wall straight up.

Iron gateposts are met on the grooved path at 1500, remnants of a vanished fence

But the great unnatural feature on this walk is the pipeline scar, which distinctly offends!

THE SUMMIT

A series of rocky knolls, on the highest of which is a cairn, adds some interest to the rather drab surroundings. It is as a viewpoint that the summit merits most respect.

DESCENTS: A quick descent to Hartsop may be made by following downhill the old wall that crosses the fellside 150 yards south-east; descents due west encounter rough ground and should not be attempted. For Patterdale the Angle Tarn path may be joined near the Satura Crag gate by following the old wall eastwards. *In bad weather, locate the wall and follow it down to the pastures of Hartsop.*

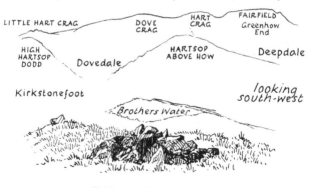

RIDGE ROUTES

Brock Crags stands apart from the ridge that links Rest Dodd with Angletarn Pikes. To join the ridge, for either of these fells, follow the old wall eastwards to the gate on Satura Crag, where the connecting path will be found.

THE VIEW

Principal Fells

The scene is interesting, with a fine surround of higher fells; in particular the bird's eye view of Brothers Water and Hartsop is beautiful and dramatic

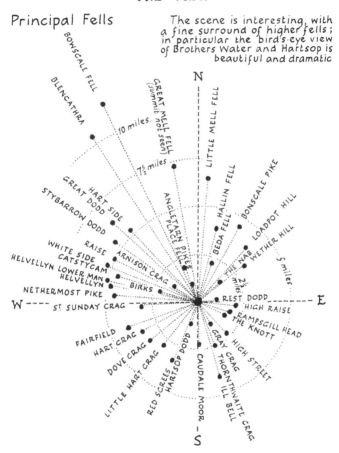

Lakes and Tarns

N : Angle Tarn
SE : Hayeswater
SW : Brothers Water
NW : Ullswater

Caudale Moor

2502'

often referred to as
John Bell's Banner
summit named
Stony Cove Pike

- Patterdale

- Hartsop

HIGH
STREET ▲
CAUDALE ▲ MOOR

▲ RED SCREES

- Ambleside

MILES
0   1   2   3   4

from Brothers Water

NATURAL FEATURES

Caudale Moor deserves far more respect than it usually gets. The long featureless slope flanking the Kirkstone Pass, well known to travellers, is not at all characteristic of the fell: its other aspects, less frequently seen, are considerably more imposing. There are, in fact, no fewer than six ridges leaving the summit in other directions, four of them of distinct merit and two of these rising to subsidiary summits, Wansfell and Hartsop Dodd, on their way to valley-level. The craggy slopes bordering the upper Troutbeck valley are particularly varied and interesting: from this remote dalehead Caudale Moor looks really impressive, especially in snowy conditions. The best single feature, however, is the formidable wall of rock, Raven Crag, overlooking Pasture Beck. Of the streams draining the fell, those to the south join forces to form Trout Beck; all others go north to feed Ullswater.

looking west

1 : *The summit (Stony Cove Pike)*
2 : *Hartsop Dodd*
3 : *St. Raven's Edge*
4 : *Main south ridge*
   continuing to Wansfell
5 : *Hart Crag*
6 : *Pike How*
7 : *Intermediate south ridge*
8 : *South ridge (east)*
9 : *North-west ridge*
10 : *North ridge*
11 : *East ridge*
12 : *Threshthwaite Mouth*
13 : *Raven Crag*
14 : *Woundale Beck*
15 : *Trout Beck*
16 : *Sad Gill*
17 : *Pasture Beck*

The six ridges of Caudale Moor

1 : North-west (*to Brothers Water*)
2 : North (*to Hartsop*)
3 : East (*to Thornthwaite Crag*
   or Hartsop or Troutbeck)
4 : South (east) (*to Troutbeck*)
5 : South (intermediate)
   (*to Troutbeck*)
6 : South (west) (*to Kirkstone*)

MAP

continuation on opposite page

MAP

ONE MILE

The word 'Low' is usually omitted in references to Hartsop village

N

PATTERDALE 2

Low Hartsop

Walker Bridge

Hayeswater Gill

old shaft

× old mine-level

Brothers Water

Threshthwaite Pasture Beck

Brotherswater Hotel

HARTSOP DODD

Caudale Bridge

sheepfold

Caudale Beck

Caudale

Raven Crag

Threshthwaite Cove

old quarry

continuation THORNTHWAITE CRAG 3

Kirkstone Beck

tarns

Threshthwaite Mouth

Mark Atkinson's Monument ×

CAUDALE MOOR (STONY COVE PIKE) 2502

continuation on opposite page

ASCENT FROM KIRKSTONE PASS
1150 feet of ascent : 2½ miles from the Inn

CAUDALE MOOR

looking north-east

monument

2400

2300

south ridge (east)

Pike How

Hart Crag

2200

2100

1900

St Ravens Edge

1800

The old zig-zag path, starting lower down the Pass, is not a regular route. It is not easy to locate: the beginning is obscure.

1700

1600

1500

1400

1300 boulder

gateway

Inn

WINDERMERE 6½

1200 cascade

1100

Kirk Stone

Kirkstone Pass

AMBLESIDE 2½

← PATTERDALE 5½

This route, with the advantage of a 1500' start, is one of the easiest ways up any of the higher fells, the only steep part being the short pull on to St Ravens Edge. It is also the *dullest* way up, and does not do justice to a fine hill that has much better than this to offer.

*Caudale Moor
from
below Scot Rake*

ASCENT FROM BROTHERS WATER
2000 feet of ascent : 2½ miles from the Hotel

CAUDALE MOOR

HARTSOP DODD

2400
2300
2200
2100
2000
1900
1800
1700
1600
1500
1400
1300
1200
1100
1000
900
800
700

Kirkstone Pass

Caudale Quarry is interesting (now disused)

Caudale Beck

path in a groove

old quarries

juniper

scree slopes

Kirkstone Beck

ruin

bracken

ruin

stone hut

Brotherswater Hotel

gate

Caudale Bridge

looking south-east

The beautiful retrospect over Patterdale is justification for frequent halts during this continuously steep ascent. The route follows the well-defined crest of the ridge. Of the many approaches to the summit, this is by far the best.

Threshthwaite Cove from Threshthwaite Mouth

ASCENT FROM TROUTBECK
2200 (A) *or* 2350 (B) *feet of ascent;*
(A) *5 miles via Sad Gill; 5½ miles via Woundale* (A)
(B) *6 miles via St Ravens Edge or Threshthwaite Mouth* (B)

looking north

Both Trout Beck
(below its attractive
slate bridge — which
few artists know but
all would love) and Sad
Gill (in several places) run
along small rocky ravines

Of the various routes
illustrated, only that
by Sad Gill (reached *via*
either side of the Tongue)
and the ridge above it
can be recommended
without qualification;
this climb has merit, but
the other routes are dull.

The valley
of the Trout Beck
west of the Tongue
is very pretty, but
the ground beyond
the bridge is wet:
the path keeps well
away from the beck.
The *east* side of the
Tongue has a dry
and excellent track

THE SUMMIT

KENTMERE PIKE   FROSWICK   ILL BELL   YOKE

The summit is a dreary plateau of considerable extent, crossed by stone walls, with grey rock outcropping in the wide expanse of grass. The highest point is not easy to locate on the flat top: it is indicated by a cairn, *east of the north-south wall*, and bears the distinctive name of Stony Cove Pike.

1: To Brothers Water
2: To Hartsop
3: To Threshthwaite Mouth
4: To Troutbeck
5: To Kirkstone

2400

grass

tarns
OD

monument

2400

grass

YARDS
0   100   200   300

N

scree

Mark Atkinson's Monument

Cairn above the north-west ridge

DESCENTS: All routes of ascent may be reversed in good weather. There are no paths on the top, but (excepting the north-west ridge) accompanying walls are safe guides from the summit.

In bad weather, note that the east face is everywhere craggy: it may be descended safely *only* by the broken wall going down to the Threshthwaite gap. The best way off the top in an emergency, whatever the destination, is alongside the wall running west — this continues without a break to the road near Kirkstone Pass Inn.

THE VIEW

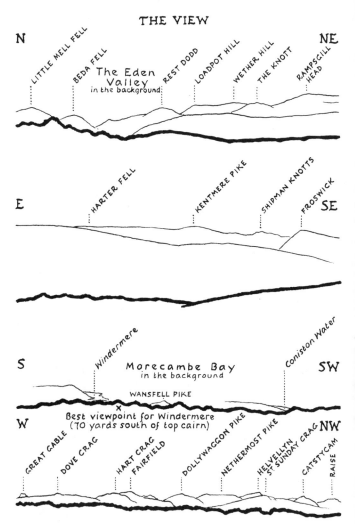

N
LITTLE MELL FELL
BEDA FELL
The Eden Valley
in the background
REST DODD
LOADPOT HILL
WETHER HILL
THE KNOTT
RAMPSGILL HEAD
NE

E
HARTER FELL
KENTMERE PIKE
SHIPMAN KNOTTS
FROSWICK
SE

S
Windermere
Morecambe Bay
in the background
WANSFELL PIKE
Coniston Water
SW

+
Best viewpoint for Windermere
(70 yards south of top cairn)

W
GREAT GABLE
DOVE CRAG
HART CRAG
FAIRFIELD
DOLLYWAGGON PIKE
NETHERMOST PIKE
HELVELLYN
St SUNDAY CRAG
CATSTYCAM
RAISE
NW

The view in this direction
is much better seen from
the western edge of the summit-plateau

THE VIEW

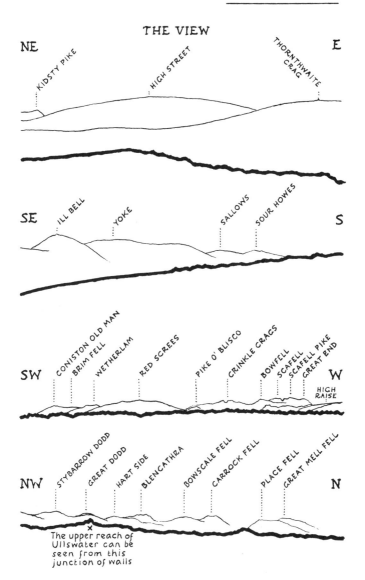

NE

KIDSTY PIKE

HIGH STREET

THORNTHWAITE CRAG

E

SE

ILL BELL

YOKE

SALLOWS

SOUR HOWES

S

SW

CONISTON OLD MAN

BRIM FELL

WETHERLAM

RED SCREES

PIKE O' BLISCO

CRINKLE CRAGS

BOWFELL

SCAFELL

SCAFELL PIKE

GREAT END

HIGH RAISE

W

NW

STYBARROW DODD

GREAT DODD

HART SIDE

BLENCATHRA

BOWSCALE FELL

CARROCK FELL

PLACE FELL

GREAT MELL FELL

N

The upper reach of
Ullswater can be
seen from this
junction of walls

RIDGE ROUTE

To WANSFELL, 1597': 4½ miles : W, then SW and S
Depression at 1100': 500 feet of ascent

A long, easy, uninteresting trudge.
For the walker who is bound
for Ambleside, with time in hand,
this route is probably best, for the
final descent from the end of the
Wansfell ridge is very beautiful—
but it must be conceded that the
intervening ground is unexciting;
moreover there are awkward walls to
climb and some marshy patches. In
mist it is better to follow the wall off
St Raven's Edge to the Kirkstone road

RIDGE ROUTES

To THORNTHWAITE CRAG, 2569′: 1 mile: ENE, then E and SE
Depression at 1950′: 620 feet of ascent
A rough scramble, safe in mist

This walk is not as simple as it looks, because the deep gap or col (Threshthwaite Mouth) between the two fells is unsuspected from the top of Caudale Moor. The descent to the gap is steep (if there is snow and ice it may be dangerous) and the climb from it is stony and loose. In mist, it is important to keep alongside the crumbled wall that links the two summits.

To HARTSOP DODD, 2018′: 1⅓ miles: N, then NNW
Depression at 1900′: 120 feet of ascent
An easy, straightforward walk

The wall running north is a dull companion to Hartsop Dodd; it is better to follow the escarpment on the right for the sake of the striking views down into Threshthwaite.

Cairn on Hart Crag above Woundale

Ullswater and Brothers Water
from Caudale Quarry

Red Screes and Middle Dodd
from the north-west ridge

Caudale Head

Raven Crag

Froswick

2359'

from Gavel Crag
(Ill Bell on the left)

▲ HIGH STREET

▲ THORNTHWAITE
CRAG

▲ FROSWICK

▲ ILL BELL

▲ YOKE

Kentmere
•

• Troutbeck

MILES
0   1   2   3   4

NATURAL FEATURES

Sheltering in the shadow of Ill Bell on High Street's south ridge is the lesser height of Froswick. It takes its pattern from Ill Bell in remarkable degree, almost humorously seeming to ape its bigger neighbour. Both flanks are very steep, the Kentmere side especially being a rough tumble of scree: there are crags here facing up the valley. The grassy Troutbeck slope, west, is notable for Froswick's one touch of originality, for it is cleft by a tremendous scree gully, Blue Gill, that splits the fellside from top to bottom. Easy slopes link the summit with Thornthwaite Crag and Ill Bell; this is the finest part of the ridge.

MAP

ASCENTS

Froswick is rarely climbed direct; invariably its summit is gained incidentally during the course of the Ill Bell ridge-walk, starting at Garburn Pass. From Troutbeck, however, its top may be visited on the way to High Street by Scot Rake, in which case it is quicker to climb alongside Blue Gill than to waste time trying to locate Scot Rake. A direct ascent from Kentmere is not recommended, this flank being steep, loose and unpleasant, although the ridge north of the summit may be reached up a continuous tongue of grass from the sheepfold.

THE SUMMIT

THORNTHWAITE CRAG

CAUDALE MOOR
Threshthwaite
Mouth

Froswick's peaked appearance from afar holds out the promise of a small pointed summit. Small it is, and neat, with a tidy cairn, but it will hardly satisfy the seeker of spires.

DESCENTS: The routes of ascent may be reversed. The western flank is safe anywhere (but keep out of Blue Gill); do not attempt the *direct* descent to Kentmere. *In mist*, reach Kentmere by way of Garburn Pass.

RIDGE ROUTES

TO THORNTHWAITE CRAG, 2569':
1 mile : NW then N and NNW
Depression at 2100': 480 feet of ascent
An easy walk on grass; safe in mist
The drawing above illustrates the route.
Incline left, at a straining post, along the
line of the old fence, of which traces remain

TO ILL BELL. 2476': ⅔ mile
S then SE
Depression at 2075': 400 feet of ascent
An easy stroll and a final scramble.
Ill Bell has a fierce appearance
on the approach, but the ascent is
not difficult. Safe in mist.

ONE MILE

THE VIEW

Sandwiched between Thornthwaite Crag
and Ill Bell, both higher, Froswick
is an undistinguished viewpoint,
the best feature being the
serrated skyline of the
Scafell and Langdale
heights in the west

Principal Fells

N

BOWSCALE FELL
BLENCATHRA
SKIDDAW
HART SIDE
GREAT DODD
STYBARROW DODD
ST SUNDAY CRAG
NETHERMOST
DOLLYWAGGON
HELVELLYN
CAUDALE MOOR
PIKE
FAIRFIELD
DOVE CRAG
PILLAR
RED SCREES
THORNTHWAITE CRAG
HIGH STREET
MARDALE ILL BELL
HARTER FELL

W — — — — — — — — — — — — E

SCAFELL PIKE
SCAFELL
BOWFELL
CRINKLE CRAGS
PIKE O' BLISCO
COLD PIKE
HARTER FELL
GREAT CARRS
SWIRL HOW
WETHERLAM
BRIM FELL
CONISTON OLD MAN

KENTMERE PIKE
SHIPMAN KNOTTS
ILL BELL
WANSFELL PIKE
TROUTBECK TONGUE
SOUR HOWES

15 miles
10 miles
5 miles

S

*Ill Bell
from
Froswick*

Lakes and Tarns
SE : Kentmere Reservoir
SSW : Windermere
NNW : Ullswater

Gray Crag

2286'

- Hartsop
- ▲ GRAY CRAG
- ▲ HIGH STREET
- ▲ THORNTHWAITE CRAG

MILES
0   1   2   3

from Hartsop

NATURAL FEATURES

A lofty ridge, bounded by exceedingly steep flanks, extends northwards from Thornthwaite Crag with a slight curve to the west, and culminates high above Hayeswater Gill in a level platform from which, on both sides, fall precipitous crags split by deep gullies. This is Gray Crag, a prominent object in the Hartsop landscape. Hayeswater forms its eastern base, while the stream issuing therefrom defines it to the north. The western boundary, below an impressive cliff of shattered rocks, is Pasture Beck.

MAP

The word 'Low' is usually omitted in references to Hartsop village

ASCENT FROM HARTSOP
1800 feet of ascent : 2 miles
(via Threshthwaite Mouth : 1950 feet of ascent : 4 miles)

THORNTHWAITE CRAG

HIGH STREET

CAUDALE MOOR

Threshthwaite Mouth

This valley above Hayeswater is not to be compared with 'Thresh'et' as a route of approach to the ridge

GRAY CRAG

sheep track

grass

marsh

Threshthwaite Cove

Raven Crag

Hayeswater

moraines

grass

dam

grass

Threshthwaite Glen

HARTSOP DODD

There is shelter among the boulders below Raven Crag

Pronounce 'Threshthwaite' *Thresh'et*

A : Hayeswater Gill
B : Pasture Beck

stile
filter house

old mine

gate

Wath Bridge

old shaft ruin

cart track

gate

gate

gate

Low Hartsop

Also illustrated in this diagram is a longer but better route — via Threshthwaite Glen to its head (or mouth!), slanting thence across to the ridge and so reaching the summit from the south. (The top of Thornthwaite Crag may easily be visited by a short detour)

looking south-south-east

The direct route climbs steeply to the ridge when free of the enclosing walls above Wath Bridge, but it is easier and more interesting to continue first to Hayeswater and gain the ridge from there.

THE SUMMIT

The summit is a pleasant level plateau of grass between steep cliffs, which should be visited for their striking downward views. DESCENTS (to Hartsop): The *only* practicable way off is by the descending north ridge, which narrows and is very enjoyable — the bilberries here are more in evidence as plants than as fruit. In *mist*, keep between the steep slopes (no rock has to be negotiated anywhere) until a plain path is reached *crossing* the fellside, and then another; *beyond these*, avoid a small crag and go down grass slopes to the Hayeswater path above Wath Bridge.

RIDGE ROUTE

To THORNTHWAITE CRAG, 2569'
1¼ miles : slightly E of S
Two minor depressions · 350 feet of ascent

A simple stroll on grass; safe in mist

Sheep tracks may be followed much of the way, but the walking is so easy that they are scarcely worth looking for. The escarpments on both flanks of the ridge are steep enough to warn of danger in mist, when it is necessary to note that *the first two walls are crossed at right angles and the third* followed.

Thornthwaite Crag from point 2331'

THE VIEW

The edges of the escarpments are better viewpoints than the cairn, the steep declivities giving remarkable depth to the scene. While the view from the western edge of the summit is the more extensive, that from the eastern reveals the most striking picture, that of Hayeswater below.

Principal Fells

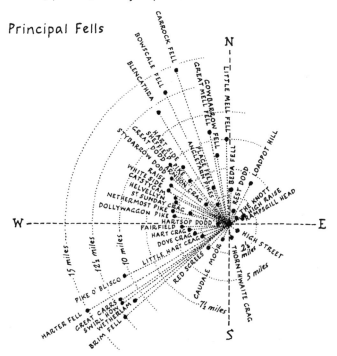

Lakes and Tarns

NNW : *Ullswater* (upper reach)

S : The small sheet of water seen above Threshthwaite Mouth is *Dubbs Reservoir*, Applethwaite Common. *Windermere* can be seen in the same direction by walking 300 yards along the ridge : it is especially well seen from point 2331. *Hayeswater* is brought into view by walking 50 yards in the direction of Rampsgill Head from the cairn, *Brothers Water* by walking 80 yards in the direction of Helvellyn.

Cascades above the filter house

Hayeswater Gill

Wath Bridge

Grey Crag

2093'

from Shipman Knotts

▲ HARTER FELL

▲ TARN CRAG
▲ KENTMERE PIKE ▲ GREY CRAG

road summit

Longsleddale Hucks Bridge

Jungle Café

Garnett Bridge Selside

MILES
0 1 2 3 4 5

NATURAL FEATURES

Shap Fells are the high link between the Pennines and Lakeland. They form a broad upland area of smooth grassy slopes and plateaux, inexpressibly wild and desolate but riven by deep valleys having each its lonely sheepfarm; gradually the ground rises in undulating ridges towards a focal point above the head of Longsleddale at the 2000-feet contour. The place of convergence of the ridges is Grey Crag, where is the first evidence, in rocky outcrops and low crags, of the characteristics so peculiar to Lakeland, although the influences of the Pennines persist in the form of peat-hags and marshes. These ridges, on a map, rather resemble the spread fingers and thumb of a hand, with Grey Crag as the palm.

IIIIIII 1500'

≡≡≡ 2000'

1 : Grey Crag
2 : Tarn Crag
3 : Capplebarrow
4 : White Howe
5 : Lords Seat
6 : Great Yarlside
7 : Wasdale Pike
8 : Seat Robert
9 : High Wether Howe

A : *Longsleddale*
B : *Bannisdale*
C : *Borrowdale*
D : *Crookdale*
E : *Wasdale*
F : *Wet Sleddale*
G : *Swindale*
H : *Mosedale*

There is nothing remarkable about Grey Crag, but here Lakeland may be said to start and moorland country to end — and the transition is sudden : the quiet beauty gives place to romantic beauty, placid scenery to exciting. One looks east, and the heart is soothed ; west, and it is stirred. Longsleddale, at the western base of the fell, is a lovely valley and, at its head, typically Lakeland. Nearby, across a slight depression north-west, is a twin height, Tarn Crag ; between them is Greycrag Tarn.

MAP

ONE MILE

continuation TARN CRAG 3

Harrop Pike

2000

1900

1800

Buck Crags

Greycrag Tarn

GREY CRAG 2093'

1900

1800

A

plantations

Galeforth Gill

survey post ×

Great Howe

fold

B
gate

Mere Crag

1700

gate

River Sprint

Brock Crag

Stockdale Beck

1600

1500
1400

1300

1200

1100

1000

C

D

Sadgill

gate

900

Brow Gill

800

Longsleddale

Stockdale

700

The Ridges leading to
the Kendal-Shap road:
A: to THE ROAD SUMMIT
         via Great Yarlside
B: to HUCKS BRIDGE
         via Lord's Seat
C: to JUNGLE CAFÉ
         via White Howe
D: to SELSIDE
         via Capplebarrow

River Sprint

600

N

GARNETT BRIDGE 4½
KENDAL-SHAP ROADS

The 2½" map of
the Ordnance
Survey states
the altitude of
Grey Crag as 2098', but other
sources agree
on 2093'

The head of Longsleddale
from Great Howe

ASCENT FROM LONGSLEDDALE
1500 feet of ascent : 1½ miles from Sadgill

GREY CRAG

TARN CRAG

Greycrag Tarn

2000
1900
1800
1700
1600
1500

Galeforth Gill

grass

survey post

TARN CRAG

Great Howe

1600
1500
1400

sheepfold

Stockdale

1300
1200
1100
1000
900
800
700

scree

Brock Crag

old quarries

bracken

easy gully

hurdle

GATESCARTH PASS

River Sprint

L o n g s l e d d a l e

A

boulders
gate   gates

gate   ruin

GARNETT BRIDGE 5

Sadgill

looking north·east

The survey post
on Great Howe
(built in connection
with the construction
of the Haweswater
Aqueduct)

The hurdle across the gap in the wall at the top of the first enclosure is awkward to negotiate, being too frail to climb. Ladies, and gentlemen with short legs, will preserve dignity best by adopting the variation start marked A, so avoiding it.

Great Howe is an excellent viewpoint for Longsleddale.

The ascent should be commenced from Sadgill Bridge, the more direct Stockdale route being much less attractive than the climb over Great Howe. The first thousand feet is steep. In mist, the ascent has nothing to commend it. No path.

ASCENTS FROM THE KENDAL-SHAP ROAD

Grey Crag may be approached from the eastern fringe
of the district along any of four clearly-defined ridges
each of which has independent and distinct summits —
and all of which descend to the main Kendal-Shap road.
These approaches are described on this and the opposite page

1 : *from*   **SELSIDE**   *and*   **JUNGLE CAFÉ**
1700 feet of ascent   1650 feet of ascent
7 miles   6 miles

GREY CRAG

Harrop Pike

Great Yarlside

These are
the two
ridges
featured
on the
opposite
page

Mere Crag

Crookdale

grass

Lords
Seat

foundation
of old wall
alongside fence

tarn

heather

Long
Crag

This Borrowdale
is not to be confused
with its famous
Cumberland
namesake

continuous fence
to Harrop Pike

grass

Bannisdale
Head

Survey column

White Howe

Borrowdale

Capplebarrow
Excellent
viewpoint

grass

heather

Bannisdale

shooting
butts

Nab
End

heathery
hummocks

stiles

hut

heather

The circuit of Bannisdale
by the ridges is itself an
excellent walk. The best
way round is clockwise,
ascending via Capplebarrow
and descending
via White Howe

gate

SHAP
8

Whiteside
Pike 1302'
— a delectable
summit of rock
and heather.
Excellent views.

tarn

gate

fields

fields

Bannisdale is concealed
from the main road by a
screen of trees and low hills.

Jungle Café

Moser
(farm)

BANNISDALE

Plough
Inn
an inspired
inn-sign!

MAIN ROAD

Longsleddale

looking north-north-west

KENDAL
5

Selside

Refer to the notes at the foot of the opposite page

ASCENTS FROM THE KENDAL-SHAP ROAD

2 : from HUCKS BRIDGE and THE ROAD SUMMIT
1700 feet of ascent   1000 feet of ascent
5 miles   5 miles

The Yarlside ridge is the easier of the two illustrated; moreover, its continuous fence makes it safe in mist.

※ STOP PRESS: The proprietors of the Eagle Nest Café have recently changed its name to Fell Top Café.

It should be noted particularly that these routes lie across very lonely territory, in striking contrast to the pulsating life and movement of the unceasing traffic on the slender ribbon of road; there are no paths along the ridges, and visitors are infrequent. The desolation is profound. Solitary walkers who want a decent burial should bear in mind that if an accident befalls them in this wilderness their bones are likely to adorn the scene until they rot and disintegrate.

These walks are more Pennine than Lakeland in character: there is very little rock but much tough grass and heather, and peat-hags and marshes are unwelcome features. Because of the nature of the ground, the traverse of the ridges should be undertaken only after a period of dry weather; they are best left alone on a wet day or during a rainy season or if under snow. Subject to the disabilities mentioned, it may be stated at once that the ridges offer easy and exhilarating walking in impressive surroundings, while the wide horizons and the vast skyscapes deserve the brush of a Turner.

This is fine open country, but it is not Lakeland.

THE SUMMIT

The top of the fell is extensive, but the highest point, indicated by a cairn, is not in doubt although it stands but little above a wide expanse of small outcrops and peat-hags.

DESCENTS: In clear weather, with ample time in hand, a way may be made to the Kendal-Shap road by any of the four ridges. If Longsleddale is the objective, the descent should be made by Great Howe in preference to a direct route via Stockdale.

In bad conditions, the descent to the Kendal-Shap road must not be undertaken lightly. Note that only the Yarlside ridge has a continuous fence or wall all the way to the road. For Longsleddale, in mist, pick a way straight down into Stockdale to avoid the scarps on Great Howe.

The cairn on Harrop Pike

Mere Crag

— a remarkably 'clean' face of rock, showing no sign of decay; lush grass grows up to its base. Climbers will enjoy its slabs.

RIDGE ROUTE
TO TARN CRAG, 2176'
¾ mile : N then NW and SSW
Depression at 1940':
250 feet of ascent

Straightforward walking, but it is better to skirt the marshes of Greycrag Tarn by keeping along the side of the fence.

HALF A MILE

THE VIEW

Grey Crag is the most easterly of the Lakeland fells, but is not of sufficient elevation to provide the panorama across the district that might be expected from its position. Higher neighbours around the head of Longsleddale conceal most of the better-known mountains, but the Coniston group is quite prominent and there is a peep of the Scafells over the saddle between Yoke and Ill Bell.

Principal Fells

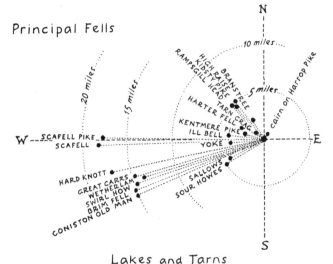

Lakes and Tarns

SSW: *Skeggles Water*
SW: *Windermere (two sections)*

Although the view towards Lakeland is disappointingly restricted, there can be no complaint of the quality of the prospects in other directions. On a clear day the panorama is remarkably extensive and very beautiful; there is a vastness, a spaciousness, about it that is usually lacking in the views from Lakeland summits. Just to the right of the cairn on Harrop Pike, Cross Fell and the twin Dun Fells start a glorious sweep of the Pennines extending south as far as Pendle Hill, with the principal heights of Mickle Fell, the Mallerstang fells, Whernside and Ingleborough all prominent. The nearer Howgill Fells, which always look attractive, are excellently grouped. Southwards is Kendal and the Kent Valley, and, beyond, Morecambe Bay silvers the horizon round to the isolated mass of Black Combe. There can be few better views in the country—but the days on which it is fully visible are also few, unfortunately.

Hallin Fell

from above Mellguards

Hallin Fell, beautifully situated overlooking a curve of Ullswater and commanding unrivalled views of the lovely secluded hinterland of Martindale, may be regarded as the motorists' fell, for the sandals and slippers and polished shoes of the numerous car-owners who park their properties on the crest of the road above the Howtown zig-zags on Sunday afternoons have smoothed to its summit a wide track that is seldom violated by the hobnails of fellwalkers. In choosing Hallin Fell as their weekend picnic-place and playground the Penrith and Carlisle motorists show commendable discrimination, for the rich rewards its summit offers are out of all proportion to the slight effort of ascent.

HALLIN FELL
• ▲
Sandwick   Howtown

PLACE   ▲ BEDA
FELL ▲   FELL

• Patterdale

MILES
0   1   2   3

MAP

Note that the scale of this map is larger than that commonly used in this book

Ullswater

Kailpot Crag

Kailpot Bay

Geordie's **Crag**

Howtown Wyke pier

Waternook

▲ HALLIN FELL 1271'

Sandwick

1100

1000

900

The Rake

Howtown Hotel

beacon

×spring

private grounds and pastures

Hallinbank

600

unenclosed road

The Hause

Church (St. Peters, Martindale)

Howegrain Beck

N

SANDWICK AND BOARDALE (road)

ONE MILE

ASCENTS

There is one royal road to the top: this is the wide grass path leaving the Hause opposite the church, and it can be ascended comfortably in bare feet; in dry weather the short smooth turf is slippery. Another track from the Hause visits the large cairn overlooking Howtown, and offers an alternative route to the top. Incidentally (although this has nothing to do with *fell*-walking!) the lakeside path *via* Kailpot Crag is entirely delightful.

HIGH RAISE RAMPSGILL HEAD THE KNOTT REST DODD GRAY CRAG CAUDALE MOOR LITTLE HART CRAG DOVE CRAG

THE NAB BEDA FELL ANGLETARN PIKES

The Martindale skyline, from the top of Hallin Fell

THE SUMMIT

The man who built the summit-cairn of Hallin Fell did more than indicate the highest point : he erected for himself a permanent memorial. This 12-foot obelisk, a landmark for miles around, is a massive structure of squared and prepared stone. The undulating top of the fell suffers from a rash of smaller, insignificant cairns : they occupy not merely the many vantage-points but even the bottoms of sundry hollows. The top is mainly grassy with bracken encroaching; there is a good deal of outcropping rock.

DESCENTS : The temptation to descend east directly to Howtown should be resisted for the slope above the Rake is rough and unpleasant.

The easiest way off, and the quickest, is by the path going down to the church on the Hause. In mist, no other route can safely be attempted.

The lower reach of Ullswater from the north cairn

THE VIEW

Principal Fells

The bird's-eye view of Ullswater is dramatic, but the classic scene unfolded is an intimate one of green fields and steep fells, the Martindale district, for which this is the best viewpoint. The panorama is good considering the modest elevation.

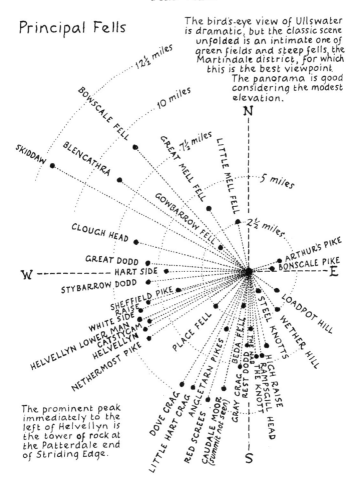

The prominent peak immediately to the left of Helvellyn is the tower of rock at the Patterdale end of Striding Edge.

Lakes and Tarns
WSW to NE : *Ullswater*
(all of the middle and lower reaches)

Harter Fell

2539'

HIGH STREET
Mardale Head ●

▲ HARTER FELL

ILL BELL ▲
▲ Kentmere PIKE

▲
SHIPMAN KNOTTS

● Kentmere

Longsleddale ●

MILES
0 1 2 3 4

from The Rigg

NATURAL FEATURES

A broad wedge of lonely upland country rises from the valley of the Kent at Burneside and continues north, narrowing, between the valleys of Kentmere and Longsleddale for nine miles; until, having very gradually attained its maximum height on Harter Fell, the ground suddenly collapses in a tremendous wall of crags, falling swiftly to the head of Mardale amongst wild and romantic surroundings — one of the noblest mountain scenes in the district. This northern face is Harter Fell's chief glory, for here, too, a shelf cradles Small Water, which is the finest of Lakeland's tarns in the opinion of many qualified to judge : seen in storm, the picture is most impressive and awe-inspiring. The other slopes have less of note although Drygrove Gill is an interesting example of landslip and Wren Gill has extensive (and dangerous) quarries. Harter Fell is one of the few fells that can claim a well-known pass on either side of its summit: Nan Bield Pass on the west and Gatescarth Pass on the east link Kentmere and Longsleddale respectively with Mardale, but since the hamlet of Mardale Head was 'drowned' by Haweswater (shame!) these passes have largely fallen from favour.

1 : The summit
2 : The Knowe
3 : Ridge continuing to Kentmere Pike
4 : Ridge continuing to Mardale Ill Bell
5 : Ridge continuing to Branstree
6 : Gatescarth Pass
7 : Nan Bield Pass
8 : Harter Fell Gully
9 : Small Water Crag
10 : Small Water
11 : Small Water Beck
12 : Gatescarth Beck
13 : Mardale Head
14 : Haweswater

looking south-east

MAP

Ull Stone from the east

continuation opposite

MARDALE ILL BELL

ONE MILE

N

Small Water Beck

shelters

Small Water

Small Water Crag

Nan Bield Pass

Black John Hole

traces of fence

HARTER FELL 2539'

broken fence

sheepfold

Dryarove Gill

The Knowe

Lingmell Gill

ILL BELL

Kentmere Reservoir

Ull Stone

Brown Howe

old quarry

continuation KENTMERE PIKE 3

fold

The Tongue

Ullstone Gill

continuation KENTMERE PIKE 3

YOKE

ford

quarries

signpost (slate slab)

Tongue Scar

sheepfold

ford

Tongue House

RIVER KENT

KENTMERE 2½ VIA HARTRIGG

KENTMERE 2¼ VIA OVEREND

MARDALE

The direction sign on the Tongue

MAP

Haweswater

road to HAWESWATER HOTEL 2½ & BAMPTON 6¼

Mardale Head

Small Water Beck

signpost

900
1000
1100
1200
1300
1400
1500
1600
1700
1800
1900
2000
2100
2200
2300
2400

sheepfold

Gatescarth Beck

Ull Stone
from the north

BRANSTREE

ONE MILE

N

traces of fence

HARTER FELL 2539

traces of fence

gate

Gatescarth Pass

2500
2400
2300
2200
2100
2000

Adam Seat

Wren Gill

1900
1800
1700
1600
1500

signpost
sheepfold

Wrengill Quarry (disused)

1800

Brown Howe

drove

fence

2300

2200

2100

2000

TARN CRAG

continuation opposite

continuation KENTMERE PIKE 3

LONGSLEDDALE SADGILL 1¾

Plan of Wrengill Quarry
(disused)

dry water race

water pipe

falls

main quarry

1
2
6
3
4
railway
ruin

secret gorge

Wren Gill

gateway
signpost

sheepfold

818

1: Stream falls into two potholes
2: Slate pillars
3: Cottages (ruins)
4: Engine shed (ruin)
5: Stream re-appears
6: Path collapsed and DANGEROUS

YARDS
0   100   200   300

The west face of Harter Fell
from the north-east ridge of Ill Bell

ASCENT FROM KENTMERE
2200 feet of ascent
5¼ miles via Nan Bield Pass :   4¼ miles via Kentmere Pike

MARDALE ILL BELL

Nan Bield Pass

HARTER FELL

2500 2400 2300

2200 2100 2000

Drygrove Gill

1900

cairned path

1800

Ull Stone

1600 1500 1400 1300 1200

Ullstone Gill

The Tongue

signpost (slate slab)

Tongue Scar

1000

sheepfold

ford

cart-track to Tongue House

old quarry

Walk north-east along the top to the third cairn for a superb full-length view of Haweswater

KENTMERE PIKE
Ordnance Survey column

Brown Howe

2300 2200 2200 grass

2000

peat hags

gap

gully

1900 1800 1700

grass

The path up the Tongue from the ford is vague. Aim for an upright slab that gives the direction (inscribed) 'To Mardale'. The more distinct path to the right leads to the quarry.

Withered Howe

gap

A detour to the cairn on Goat Scar is recommended in clear weather: (see Kentmere Pike 4)

1300

See Kentmere Pike 4 for fuller details of the Hollowbank route

At Overend, take the upper grass path, not the cart-track.

Overend

River Kent

Hollow-bank

groove

crag ruins

gate

1100 1000

Tongue Scar is a natural habitat of badgers and foxes, and the whole valley is rich in wild life

looking north

KENTMERE 1½ (grass lane)

KENTMERE 1½ (road)

When selecting the route of ascent on a misty day, note that it is easier to locate the top of Harter Fell by the ridge from Nan Bield Pass than it is to find Nan Bield Pass from the top of Harter Fell.

Two routes are shown. That from Hollowbank is both easier and shorter, that from Overend much the more beautiful and interesting. The round journey serves as an excellent introduction to upper Kentmere. The sharp-crested Nan Bield is the finest of Lakeland passes.

ASCENT FROM LONGSLEDDALE
1950 feet of ascent : 4¼ miles from Sadgill

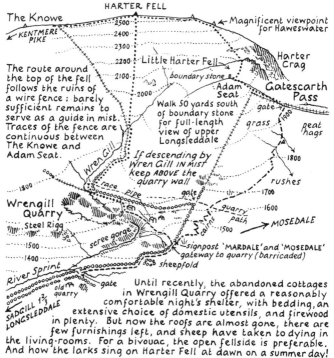

HARTER FELL

The Knowe

← KENTMERE PIKE

← Magnificent viewpoint for Haweswater

2500
2400
2300
2200
2100
2000

Little Harter Fell
boundary stone

Harter Crag

Adam Seat

Gatescarth Pass

gate
grass
peat hags

1900

The route around the top of the fell follows the ruins of a wire fence: barely sufficient remains to serve as a guide in mist. Traces of the fence are continuous between The Knowe and Adam Seat.

Walk 50 yards south of boundary stone for full-length view of upper Longsleddale

If descending by Wren Gill IN MIST keep ABOVE the quarry wall

1800

Wren Gill

race pipe

gate

1800

1700
rushes

Wrengill Quarry
Steel Rigg

scree gorge

1500
1400

quarry path
cairns

1500

1600

→ MOSEDALE

River Sprint

old quarry

SADGILL 1⅔
LONGSLEDDALE

gate

signpost 'MARDALE' and 'MOSEDALE'
gateway to quarry (barricaded)

sheepfold

Until recently, the abandoned cottages in Wrengill Quarry offered a reasonably comfortable night's shelter, with bedding, an extensive choice of domestic utensils, and firewood in plenty. But now the roofs are almost gone, there are few furnishings left, and sheep have taken to dying in the living-rooms. For a bivouac, the open fellside is preferable. And how the larks sing on Harter Fell at dawn on a summer day!

The disappearance of Wren Gill

looking north-west

The Gatescarth route is particularly easy: a hands-in-pockets stroll with no steep climbing, the top being reached with surprising lack of effort. Nonagenarians will find it eminently suitable.
Avoid Wren Gill in mist.

ASCENT FROM MARDALE
1750 feet of ascent : 2 miles from the road end

looking south

The round journey is recommended, ascending by Gatescarth and returning by Nan Bield and Small Water in order to keep the best views in front. To locate the ridge going down to Nan Bield from the highest cairn walk in the direction of Red Screes. Strangers to Harter Fell should keep off it in bad weather.

The pattern of Manchester Corporation's Haweswater signposts

This is an excellent expedition, richly rewarding in intimate scenes of Harter Fell's grand northern cliffs and in the views of Haweswater from its summit, yet short in distance and needing much less effort in execution than its formidable appearance suggests.

THE SUMMIT

HIGH STREET

MARDALE
ILL BELL

A mild shock awaits anyone reaching the top of the fell on a first visit, especially in mist, for there is a spectral weirdness about the two highest cairns. The stones support an elaborate superstructure of iron fence-posts and railings, which, having served their original mission, now act as an adornment that has a nightmarish quality.

The highest part of the fell, a graceful curve, is a long grassy sheep-walk. The fence that formerly traversed its length is now in complete ruin, but can still be traced, and is followed by the pedestrian route across the top. As so often on easy ground, no paths have been trodden out, and only occasionally does a faint track materialise.

The altitude of Harter Fell is variously stated by different authorities as 2509', 2539', 2560' and 2585'. The Ordnance Survey figure of 2539' is reliable.

crags
2300

In mist, note change of direction in fence at third cairn

traces of fence

boundary stone (fallen) inscribed 'L'

2400
2500
grass
traces of fence

YARDS
0   100   200   300

A: to Nan Bield Pass
B: to Kentmere Pike
C: to Wren Gill, for Longsleddale
D: to Gatescarth Pass

A ←---
peat bed (sometimes a shallow tarn)

straining post
C

grass
B

DESCENTS: Some difficulty arises in locating the ridge going down west to Nan Bield Pass, which cannot be seen from the summit. The top of the ridge is quickly reached by proceeding directly from the highest cairn towards Red Screes. Other routes follow the fence, although a quick way down to Wren Gill may also be noted.

In mist, aim for the Nan Bield ridge from the straining-post near the top cairn, passing between the cairn (right) and peat bed (left). Keep to the line of the fence on other routes.

Haweswater
from the third cairn

THE VIEW

THE VIEW

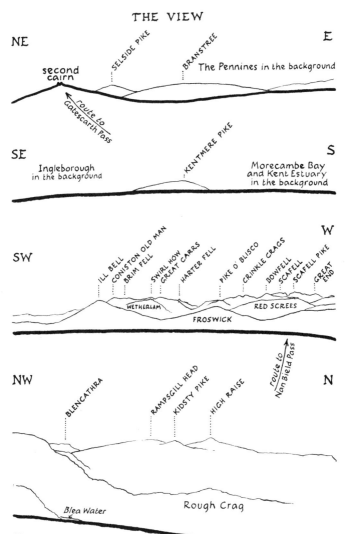

NE

second cairn

SELSIDE PIKE

BRANSTREE

The Pennines in the background

E

route to Gatescarth Pass

SE

Ingleborough in the background

KENTMERE PIKE

Morecambe Bay and Kent Estuary in the background

S

SW

ILL BELL
CONISTON OLD MAN
BRIM FELL
SWIRL HOW
GREAT CARRS
HARTER FELL
PIKE O' BLISCO
CRINKLE CRAGS
BOWFELL
SCAFELL
SCAFELL PIKE
GREAT END

WETHERLAM

RED SCREES

FROSWICK

W

NW

BLENCATHRA

RAMPSGILL HEAD
KIDSTY PIKE

HIGH RAISE

route to Nan Bield Pass

N

Blea Water

Rough Crag

Blea Water cannot be seen from
the cairn, but is brought into view by walking a few yards north-west.

RIDGE ROUTES

To BRANSTREE, 2333': 2 miles : NE then SE and NE
Depression at 1875' (Gatescarth Pass) : 465 feet of ascent
An easy walk on grass, tedious beyond Gatescarth

Follow the line of the old fence around the watershed to the good fence on Adam Seat: this runs unbroken across Gatescarth Pass and up to the top of Branstree. *In mist*, it is important to note the sharp angle in the route at the third cairn: crags are ahead.

To KENTMERE PIKE, 2397': 1¼ miles
S then SSE
Depression at 2275' : 150 feet of ascent
A simple stroll on grass

Walk south along the level top until the fence becomes more pronounced, then follow it — an intermittent path accompanies it on the right.

Boundary stone on Adam Seat

RIDGE ROUTE

To MARDALE ILL BELL, 2496′: W, then WNW and NW
1 mile

Depression at 2100′(Nan Bield Pass): 450 feet of ascent
An excellent crossing of a fine pass, with beautiful and impressive views
Aim west (in the direction of Red Screes) until the ridge going down
to Nan Bield is seen below: this is a delectable descent, Small Water
being a striking feature. Nan Bield is marked by a big cairn-shelter;
round the outcrop beyond on the left side. Slant up to the right over
rough ground when the path fades and watch for the white boulders
that indicate the final rise to the summit. *In mist, Mardale Ill Bell
is confusing and dangerous ; there are no paths across the top.*

Small Water

Hartsop Dodd

• Patterdale

• Hartsop

▲ HARTSOP DODD

▲ CAUDALE MOOR

MILES
0 1 2 3 4

from Goldrill Beck

NATURAL FEATURES

For a few miles along the road from Patterdale to Kirkstone, Hartsop Dodd has the form of a steepsided conical hill, rising like a giant tumulus from the flat floor of the valley; a high ridge connecting with the loftier Caudale Moor behind is unseen and unsuspected. After the fashion of many subsidiary fells in this area, the imposing front is a sham, for the Dodd is no more than the knuckled fist at the end of one of the several arms of Caudale Moor. It rises from pleasant places, pastures and woods and water, and quite rightly has been named from the delightful hamlet nestling unspoilt among trees at its foot.

MAP

It is interesting to note that Hartsop Dodd (*Low* Hartsop Dodd) has a greater elevation than its counterpart *High* Hartsop Dodd nearby, the prefixes relating to their geographical positions in the valley, not to their altitudes

The word 'Low' is usually omitted in references to Hartsop village

continuation CAUDALE MOOR 3

ASCENTS

A feature of the paths leading up Hartsop Dodd is that, for much of their length, they run in well-engineered grooves that help considerably in defining the routes. The best way up is by the steep north ridge, a beautiful climb. The path zigzagging up the west flank is also steep, and rather dreary. The only easy route follows Caudale Beck at first and ultimately gains the ridge between the Dodd and Caudale Moor; this way is dull.

THE SUMMIT

A wall crosses the grassy top, the highest point being indicated by a wooden fence-post against the wall from which a fence formerly went down the fellside. A few stones fallen from the wall at its first bend southwards have been piled together to form a cairn of no significance.

High Raise · Rampsgill Head · Gray Crag · The Knott

RIDGE ROUTE

HARTSOP DODD

1900
2000
2100
2200
2300
2400

Raven Crag

Threshthwaite Cove

CAUDALE MOOR

ONE MILE

N

DESCENTS: The grooves do not continue onto the summit. To find the path going down to the west, walk in the direction of Dove Crag, passing by two more fence-posts minus fence — the top of the groove is just beyond the second. To find the path down the north ridge walk towards Ullswater — the groove starts soon after the ground steepens; keep to the ridge and avoid the parallel gully on the right. The longer easy route is scarcely worth consideration.

In mist, the path on the west will be easiest to find — leave the top fence-post at right angles to the wall and look for the other two which give the key to the descent.

To CAUDALE MOOR, 2502'
1½ miles : SSE, then S
Depression at 1900' : 620 feet of ascent

An easy climb on grass, safe in mist. The wall drearily links the two summits. In fine weather, interest may be introduced into the walk by following the edge of the escarpment on the left, the views therefrom down into Threshthwaite being very striking.

THE VIEW

The view of Dove Crag and Dovedale across the gulf of the Patterdale valley is exceedingly impressive, a classic amongst views. Red Screes, too, rises majestically and steeply from the depths of Kirkstone. The edges of the summit, rather than the top, give the best views.

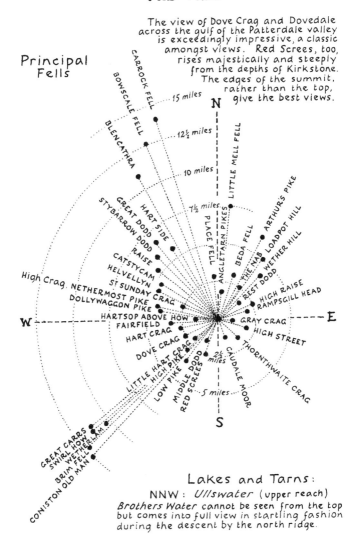

Principal Fells

Lakes and Tarns:

NNW: *Ullswater* (upper reach)
Brothers Water cannot be seen from the top but comes into full view in startling fashion during the descent by the north ridge.

Dovedale

Patterdale

High Raise

2634'

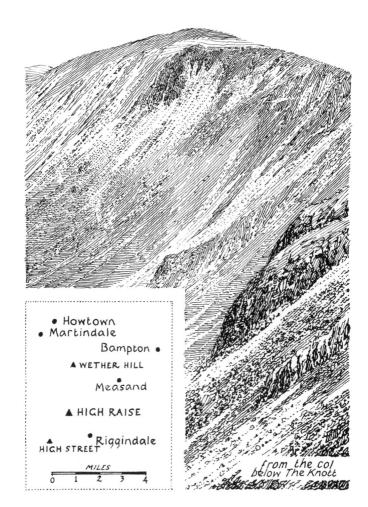

Howtown
Martindale
Bampton
▲ WETHER HILL
Measand
▲ HIGH RAISE
▲ HIGH STREET • Riggindale

MILES
0 1 2 3 4

from the col
below The Knott

NATURAL FEATURES

Second in altitude among the fells east of Kirkstone and Ullswater, High Raise is overtopped only by High Street itself. Topographically, it cannot be said to occupy an important position, for it commands no valleys and it is not a meeting-place of ridges; yet, nevertheless, its summit-cone rises distinctively from the lofty watershed of the main range, and it is the last fell, going north, with the characteristics of a mountain — beyond are rolling foothills. Flanking it on the west is the valley of Rampsgill, to which falls abruptly a featureless wall of grass and scree. Much more extensive, and much more interesting, are the eastern declivities, going down to Haweswater: here natural forces have scooped out a great hollow just below the subsidiary summit of Low Raise, leaving a mile-long fringe of crags between two airy ridges. There are considerable streams on this flank, and all flow into Haweswater. Formerly these waters helped to irrigate the fertile Lowther and Eden valleys, but nowadays only the most favoured do so: the fate of the majority is captive travel along less pleasurable routes to the taps of Manchester, there to serve the needs of man in other ways.

looking south

1 : The summit   2 : Low Raise   3 : Raven Howe   4 : Red Crag
5 : Ridge continuing to Rampsgill Head   6 : Ridge continuing to Wether Hill
7 : South-east ridge   8 : North-east ridge   9 : Birks Crag
10 : Whelter Crags   11 : Lad Crags   12 : Haweswater
13 : Whelter Beck   14 : Measand Beck   15 : Longgrain Beck
16 : Keasgill Head   17 : Redcrag Tarn   18 : Rampsgill Beck

MAP

Rampsgill is within the Martindale Deer Forest.
There are no public paths in this valley.

ONE MILE

MAP

ASCENTS FROM PATTERDALE AND HARTSOP
2400 feet of ascent : 5¼ miles from Patterdale
2250 feet of ascent : 3½ miles from Hartsop

The brief view down
Bannerdale from
Satura Crag is often
missed. Detour left
of the path to see it.

The valley down on
the right is that of
Hayeswater Gill : it
descends to Hartsop.

For a diagram of the
path from Hartsop
see The Knott 3

For a diagram of the ascent
to Angle Tarn from Patterdale
see Angletarn Pikes 5

looking east

   This is a most enjoyable excursion with a succession
of widely differing views, all excellent; and the route
itself, never very distinct, is an interesting puzzle to
unravel. In bad weather, however, there will be some
difficulty, and a stranger may run into trouble on top
of Rampsgill Head, where there are crags.

ASCENT FROM MARTINDALE
2100 feet of ascent : 5 miles from Martindale (Old Church)

In a few places, notably just beyond the ruined hut, the path is indistinct, but on a clear day the direction is always obvious. This is a safe walk in mist for anyone familiar with the lay of the land. In bad weather the hut is a landmark of some importance and a key to one's whereabouts.

From Howtown, the hut may be reached more quickly by a direct route along Fusedale.

looking south-south-east

As an alternative route for return, good walkers are recommended to continue over Rampsgill Head and work round to Angle Tarn, whence a descent may be made along Bannerdale or, at the cost of a little more energy, along the Beda ridge : a fine walk.

This is the only full-size mountain expedition conveniently available from the neighbourhood of Martindale and Howtown. It hardly lives up to its early promise, the middle section being dull, but the views are excellent throughout.

ASCENTS FROM MARDALE
1900 feet of ascent
2½ miles from Riggindale; 3½ miles from Measand

looking west

Note that the starting-points of
the climbs illustrated are considerable
distances from habitations (Riggindale is
3½ miles from the Haweswater Hotel; Measand is 3 miles
from Bampton). If returning to Mardale from the summit, these
distances will again have to be traversed at the end of the day and
will then seem even longer.

The zig-zag path at the foot of the south-east ridge went out of use
when the nearby buildings were submerged, and is now difficult to
find and follow. All who ascend by this route are recommended to
make a small detour to visit the remains of the ancient fort, which,
crag-defended and double-moated, occupied a striking position, and
even today its ruins are a stimulus to the imagination.

The routes depicted are unfrequented and without
paths except initially. All are interesting, and the
south-east ridge especially is an attractive climb.

Haweswater, from Measand
at the foot of the north-east ridge

The British Fort
on the south-east ridge
*with Haweswater **beyond***

THE SUMMIT

BRANSTREE TARN CRAG Gatescarth Pass HARTER FELL Nan Bield Pass MARDALE ILL BELL

The true fell-walker appreciates best a summit with rocks; failing that, a summit with stones. He will, therefore, have an affectionate regard for High Raise, especially if his visit follows a tour of the neighbouring fells, for its top is crowned with stones in a quantity uncommon amongst the heights of the High Street range, which are usually grassy — they are rough, weathered and colourful stones, a pleasure to behold. Some have been used in the erection of a large cairn; others form an effective wind-shelter alongside. The old High Street, here merely a narrow track, crosses the top below the cap of stones, 100 yards west of the cairn. It is the only path.

A long half-mile away, slightly north of east, is the rounded hump of Low Raise. Here all is grass except for a remarkable oasis of bleached stones, obviously transported — a tumulus. These stones were a convenient quarry for later generations whose preference it was to build cairns rather than tumuli, and a really handsome edifice has been constructed.

*The tumulus and cairn
on Low Raise*

DESCENTS

Since the friendly inn and farmsteads of Mardale were so cruelly sacrificed for the common good (*sic*), the summit of High Raise has been remote from tourist accommodation. It should be noted that the only beds in Mardale nowadays are concentrated in the new Haweswater Hotel, which, for walkers, is sited on the wrong side of the lake, and which, unlike the old Dun Bull, is much more a motorists' resort than a refuge for foot-travellers and shepherds.

Ample time should be allowed for descents, which are lengthy in all directions, and confusing in all directions except to the east, especially so in bad weather.

The natural inclination to scramble down into Rampsgill must be resisted : this valley offers sanctuary for deer, and there is neither welcome nor lodging for two-legged animals.

Descents should not be made in the areas shaded

To PATTERDALE : An interesting and beautiful walk in good weather, but an anxious and complicated journey in bad. Note that Rampsgill Head must first be climbed before the descent properly commences, and that The Knott is rounded on its north side. *In bad weather, after crossing the wall between The Knott and Rest Dodd, descend directly to Hayeswater and Hartsop.*

To MARDALE : The north-east ridge particularly is a good way down, and the best if Bampton is the objective. The south-east ridge is rougher, with excellent views, but leads only to the uninhabited head of the valley : for the Haweswater Hotel, however, it is a useful route. *In mist, the streams are safe guides to the lakeside, but care is needed along Measand Beck.*

To MARTINDALE, HOWTOWN and POOLEY BRIDGE : Follow the ridge north, turning down left at Keasgill Head for Martindale and Howtown — and, in bad weather, for Pooley Bridge also. Consult the Wether Hill map.

THE VIEW

THE VIEW

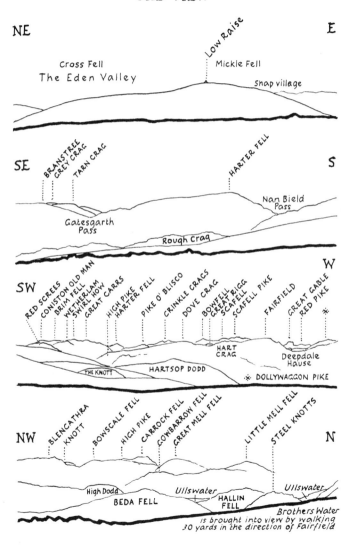

is brought into view by walking
30 yards in the direction of Fairfield

RIDGE ROUTES

To WETHER HILL, 2210' : 2¼ miles : NNE
Depression at 2150' : 100 feet of ascent
A long easy walk, safe in mist

Facing north, incline left to join the path (the old High Street), which continues, but not distinctly, to Wether Hill and beyond. It is usual to keep to the left of the wall as far as Redcrag Tarn and then cross it, but it is quicker, and in bad weather better, to follow it on the right. At the depression of Keasgill Head the path is badly cut away by a series of shallow ravines. Wether Hill has two tops; the cairn is on the furthest.

Redcrag Tarn
looking to High Raise and Rampsgill Head

To RAMPSGILL HEAD, 2581'
¾ mile : SW
Depression at 2450':
140 feet of ascent
Easy, but needing care in mist

Join and follow the path to the grassy depression south-west. Here is a bifurcation : take the right fork and detour to look down the crags. In mist, keep left, on easy ground, if crags are encountered.

Whelter Beck and Whelter Crags

High Street

2718'

from the north ridge of Branstree

NATURAL FEATURES

Most of the high places in Lakeland have no mention in history books, and, until comparatively recent times, when enlightened men were inspired to climb upon them for pleasure and exercise, it was fashionable to regard them as objects of awe and terror, and their summits were rarely visited. Not so High Street, which has been known and trodden, down through the ages, by a miscellany of travellers on an odd variety of missions: by marching soldiers, marauding brigands, carousing shepherds, officials of the Governments, and now by modern hikers. Its summit has been in turn a highway and a sports arena and a racecourse, as well as, as it is today, a grazing ground for sheep.

The long whale-backed crest of High Street attains a greater altitude than any other fell east of Kirkstone. Walking is easy on the grassy top: a factor that must have influenced the Roman surveyors to throw their road along it. But High Street is much more than an elevated and featureless field, for its eastern flank, which falls precipitously from the flat top to enclose the splendid tarn of Blea Water in craggy arms, is a striking study in grandeur and wildness; on this side a straight narrow ridge running down to Mardale is particularly fine. The western face drops roughly to Hayeswater. To north and south, high ground continues to subsidiary fells along the main ridge.

Rough Crag from Long Stile

The River Kent has its birth in marshes on the south slope but most of the water draining from the fell flows northwards to Haweswater and Hayeswater.

High Street 3

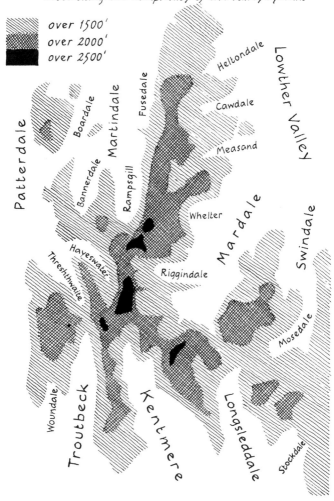

NATURAL FEATURES

The main High Street range
illustrating the complexity of the valley systems

over 1500'
over 2000'
over 2500'

Patterdale

Boardale

Martindale

Bannerdale

Rampsgill

Fusedale

Heltondale

Cawdale

Lowther Valley

Measand

Whelter

Mardale

Swindale

Hayeswater

Riggindale

Threshthwaite

Mosedale

Woundale

Troutbeck

Kentmere

Longsleddale

Stockdale

MAP

HARTSOP 1

Hayeswater

moraines

continuation
THE KNOTT 2

continuation
RAMPSGILL HEAD 4

gateway

ROMAN ROAD

Twopenny Crag

Straits of Riggindale

Short Stile

continuation below

Long Stile

Ordnance Survey column
HIGH STREET
2718

Blea Water Crag

Blea Water

ONE MILE

N

1400
1500
1600
1700
1800
1900
2000
2100
2200
2300
2400
2500
2600
2700

continuation
MARDALE ILL BELL 4

continuation
THORNTHWAITE CRAG 3

continuation above

sheepfold

Riggindale Beck

Haweswater

The Rigg

Caspel Gate

tarn

Rough Crag

Eagle Crag

Heron Crag

Haweswater

road to
HAWESWATER
HOTEL 2½

Blea Water

sheepfold

Blea Water Beck

Dodderwick Force

stiles

signpost

Mardale Head

ASCENTS FROM PATTERDALE AND HARTSOP
2450 feet of ascent : 5½ miles from Patterdale
2300 feet of ascent : 3¾ miles from Hartsop

Proceed from the Straits of Riggindale to the summit
not by the wall nor by the Roman Road (which are
dull trudges) but by following the edge of the eastern
face (which has excellent views) until the Ordnance
Survey column comes into sight.

HIGH STREET

RAMPSGILL HEAD

Straits of Riggindale

ROMAN ROAD

2700   2600   2500   2400   2300

2500   2400   grass

Rampsgill

REST DODD

THE KNOTT

tarn

gateway

groove

2300   2200

2200   2100   2000   1900   1800

scree gully

Enterprising pedestrians
approaching from Hartsop
may tackle High Street
direct from the head
of Hayeswater — but
they will not enjoy
the climb, which is
steep, dull, and
overburdened
with
scree

2200   2100   2000

peat hags

1900

grass

Bannerdale

1900   1800   1700   1600

Satura Crag

Buck Crag

1800   1700   1600

gate

BROCK CRAGS

1700   1600   1500   1400   moraines

Hayeswater

dam

gate

HARTSOP

For a diagram
of the path from
Hartsop to Hayeswater
see The Knott 3

Angle Tarn

For a diagram
of the ascent
to Angle Tarn
from Patterdale
see Angletarn Pikes 5

PATTERDALE 2

looking south-east

Two good viewpoints, only a few paces from the
path but often missed, are (1) the main cairn on
Satura Crag (view of Bannerdale), and (2) the tarn
on the col below Rampsgill Head (view of Rampsgill)

This is the least exciting approach to High Street; it
is, nevertheless, a very enjoyable walk, with a series
of varied and beautiful views; and the tracking of
the indistinct path, which has many unexpected
turns and twists, is interesting throughout.

ASCENT FROM MARDALE
2050 feet of ascent   3 miles from the road end

HIGH STREET

2600   2700

2500   Blea Water Crag

2400

steep
scree slopes

Long Stile

Blea Water

Caspel Gate
tarn

Riggindale

Caspel Gate is
the name of
a grassy
depression 1500
on the ridge:
there is no gate.
The tarn
there
dries up
in times
of drought.

sheepfold

grass slope

Rough Crag

1900

1800   Eagle
Crag

1700   1600   Heron
Crag

1400

Blea Water Beck

boulders

stile

1300

1500

The ridge route may
safely be attempted
in mist, being so
well-defined that
it is impossible to
go astray—but it
should be kept in
mind that there
are crags close by
on both sides for
most of the route,
the Riggindale
flank (north) in
particular being
precipitous.

Dodderwick Force

NAN BIELD PASS

Swine
Crag

bracken

1000

BURN BANKS

Mardale
Head

signpost ×

Haweswater

Haweswater

Although a
rather easier
alternative via
Blea Water is
illustrated, it is
a poor substitute
for the ridge. Use it,
however, when descending
from the summit in bad weather.

HAWESWATER
HOTEL (road) 2½

The Rigg

looking west

The ridge of Rough Crag and the rocky stairway of
Long Stile together form the connoisseur's route up
High Street, the only route that discloses the finer
characteristics of the fell. The ascent is a classic,
leading directly along the crest of a long, straight
ridge that permits of no variation from the valley
to the summit. The views are excellent throughout.

ASCENT FROM TROUTBECK
2350 feet of ascent : 6 miles

THORNTHWAITE CRAG

HIGH STREET

Threshthwaite Mouth

FROSWICK

ILL BELL

GARBURN

SCOT RAKE (ROMAN ROAD)

Blue Gill

via Threshthwaite Mouth

HARTSOP

gate

TROUTBECK TONGUE

quarry

gate

gate

quarry

gate   gate

gate

Troutbeck Park Farm

Trout Beck

Hagg Gill

WINDERMERE

gate

TROUTBECK 1½ (farm road)

The fine mountain on the left of this valley-head is Caudale Moor

High Street cannot be seen from the Troutbeck valley, nor does it come into sight on the approach until Thornthwaite Crag has been rounded. The last mile lacks interest. Do not omit the small detour eastwards from the top to the edge of the cliffs to look down on Mardale.

Strong walkers are recommended, as an alternative (and far more exhilarating) route of ascent, to approach via the Ill Bell ridge from Garburn Pass.

Scot Rake, rising in a series of grooves across the breast of Froswick, is more easily discerned from a distance than when it is actually sought on the fell. To locate it from the angle in the wall, go straight up the slope and turn left above a small landslide to a groove which may be followed (with some doubts) until the path becomes visible as it climbs the fell ahead.

When the ridge is reached above Scot Rake there is an excellent view, looking back, of Ill Bell and Froswick — this is one of the best mountain scenes in the district.

looking north

The route illustrated is the *direct* way and is easy and pleasant throughout, steep only on the initial part of the climb to the ridge. It is safe in mist, and a very quick route when used for descent.

ASCENT FROM KENTMERE
2300 feet of ascent
5½ miles via Hall Cove : 6 miles via Nan Bield Pass

looking
north-north-west

Consult
Mardale Ill Bell 6
& Thornthwaite Crag 6
for additional
notes on the routes
illustrated

This is the usual route
to Nan Bield from
Kentmere (for
details of the start
see Harter Fell 6)

High Street is commonly
ascended from Kentmere by
way of the Ill Bell ridge (the best
route) or *via* Mardale Ill Bell, but it
may be climbed direct from Hall Cove
(or by a variation over Gavel Crag):
an interesting expedition.

Haweswater, from above Long Stile

Hayeswater, from the Roman Road

THE SUMMIT

The summit is barren of scenic interest, and only visitors of lively imagination will fully appreciate their surroundings. Any person so favoured may recline on the turf and witness, in his mind's eye, a varied pageant of history, for he has been preceded here, down the ages, by the ancient Britons who built their villages and forts in the valleys around; by the Roman cohorts marching between their garrisons at Ambleside and Brougham; by the Scots invaders who were repulsed on the Troutbeck slopes; by the shepherds, dalesmen and farmers who, centuries ago, made the summit their playground and feasting-place on the occasion of their annual meets; by racing horses (the summit is still named Racecourse Hill on the large-scale Ordnance Survey maps).....and let us not forget Dixon of immortal legend, whose great fall over the cliff while fox-hunting is an epic in enthusiasm.

Nowadays all is quiet here and only the rising larks disturb the stillness. A pleasant place, but — to those unfortunate folk with no imagination — so dull!

DESCENTS should be made only by the regular routes. It must be emphasised that there is only one direct way to Mardale — by Long Stile, the top of which is indicated by a cairn. Direct descents into Kentmere may lead to trouble, the best plan being to aim for Nan Bield Pass, in clear weather.

In mist, consult the maps. For Mardale, stick to the crest of Long Stile, but at Caspel Gate turn down right to Blea Water. Kentmere is best reached by descending into Hall Cove at a point 100 yards south-east of the end of the High Street wall. Avoid the Hayeswater face.

M: Mardale
K: Kentmere
T: Troutbeck
H: Hartsop
P: Patterdale

Blea Water

Do not attempt descents in areas shaded

THE VIEW

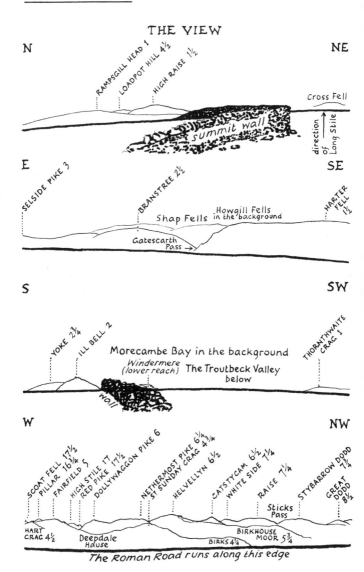

N · NE

RAMPSGILL HEAD 1 · LOADPOT HILL 4½ · HIGH RAISE 1½

Cross Fell

summit wall

direction of Long Stile →

E · SE

SELSIDE PIKE 3 · BRANSTREE 2½

Shap Fells · Howgill Fells in the background

HARTER FELL 1½

Gatescarth Pass →

S · SW

YOKE 2¾ · ILL BELL 2

Morecambe Bay in the background
Windermere (lower reach) · The Troutbeck Valley below

THORNTHWAITE CRAG 1

wall

W · NW

SCOAT FELL 17½ · PILLAR 16¾ · FAIRFIELD 5 · HIGH STILE 17 · RED PIKE 17½ · DOLLYWAGGON PIKE 6 · NETHERMOST PIKE 6½ · ST SUNDAY CRAG 4¼ · HELVELLYN 6½ · CATSTYCAM 6½ · WHITE SIDE 7¼ · RAISE 7¼ · STYBARROW DODD 7¾ · GREAT DODD 8½

HART CRAG 4½ · Deepdale Hause · BIRKS 4¼ · BIRKHOUSE MOOR 5¾ · Sticks Pass

The Roman Road runs along this edge

THE VIEW

NE   E

The figures following the names of fells
indicate distances in miles

The Pennines in the background

View of Haweswater and Blea Water from this edge

SE   S

Ingleborough   KENTMERE PIKE 2½   MARDALE ILL BELL ¾

Morecambe Bay
and the Kent Estuary

The Kentmere Valley
below

SW   W

CONISTON OLD MAN 13¼
BRIM FELL 13
SWIRL HOW 12¼
GREAT CARRS 12¼
RED SCREES 3
HARTER FELL 15½
PIKE O' BLISCO 11½
CRINKLE CRAGS 12½
BOWFELL 12½
SCAFELL 14¾
SCAFELL PIKE 14¼
GREAT END 13½
GREAT GABLE 14¾

CAUDALE MOOR 1½   DOVE CRAG 4

The Roman Road runs along this edge

NW   N

SKIDDAW 15¾
HART SIDE 7¼
ANGLETARN PIKES 3
BLENCATHRA 12½
PLACE FELL 4¼
BOWSCALE FELL 13¾
HIGH PIKE 16½
CARROCK FELL 15¼
REST DODD ¾
GREAT MELL FELL 9¼
THE KNOTT 1
BEDA FELL 4
LITTLE MELL FELL 8

View of Hayeswater from this edge

RIDGE ROUTES

To RAMPSGILL HEAD, 2581′: 1¼ miles: N then NE
Depression at 2340′: 250 feet of ascent
An easy and interesting walk

Follow the edge of the escarpment north to the narrow Straits of Riggindale. Beyond, watch for the divergence to the right from the main path, and bear left when the top of the fell is reached.

To MARDALE ILL BELL, 2496′:
⅘ mile: SE then ESE
Depression at 2350′: 150 feet of ascent
An easy walk with fine views

Follow the edge of the escarpment south-east —a cairn en route indicates an excellent view of Blea Water. Incline left when the marshy depression is crossed. In mist, there is likely to be some uncertainty beyond the depression.

To THORNTHWAITE CRAG, 2569′
1¼ miles: SW then W and NW
Depression at 2475′
100 feet of ascent
A simple stroll, safe in mist

The mile to the end of the wall on Thornthwaite Crag is a very 'quick' one, the gentle gradient inducing speed —and there is little of interest to detain the walker. In clear weather, a short 'cut' may be used to avoid the final semi-circle.

High Street from Mardale Ill Bell

Blea Water Crag

Ill Bell

2476'

named 'Hill Bell' on the
2½" Ordnance Survey map

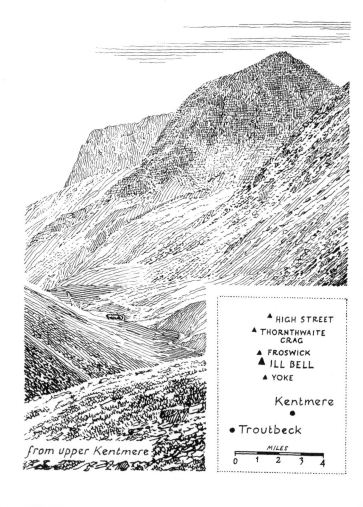

from upper Kentmere

▲ HIGH STREET

▲ THORNTHWAITE
CRAG

▲ FROSWICK

▲ ILL BELL

▲ YOKE

Kentmere
●

● Troutbeck

MILES
0 1 2 3 4

NATURAL FEATURES

The graceful cone of Ill Bell is a familiar object to most residents of south Westmorland and those visitors who approach Lakeland by way of Kendal and Windermere, although few who know it by sight can give it a name and fewer still its correct name. It is the dominating height on a steep-sided ridge, running north to High Street from the foothills of Garburn, and forms a most effective and imposing barrier between the Troutbeck and upper Kentmere valleys. It is linked by easy slopes to its neighbours, Yoke and Froswick, but both flanks are excessively steep: the Kentmere side in particular is very rough and the aspect of the fell from the upper reaches of the valley is magnificent. Crags descend northwards from the small summit. Ill Bell is distinctive and of good appearance, its peaked shape making it easily identifiable. The ridge on which it stands is probably the most popular fell-walk east of Kirkstone.

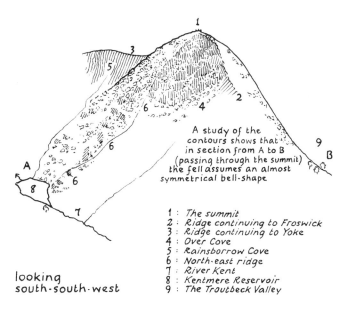

A study of the contours shows that in section from A to B (passing through the summit) the fell assumes an almost symmetrical bell-shape

1 : The summit
2 : Ridge continuing to Froswick
3 : Ridge continuing to Yoke
4 : Over Cove
5 : Rainsborrow Cove
6 : North-east ridge
7 : River Kent
8 : Kentmere Reservoir
9 : The Troutbeck Valley

looking
south-south-west

Ill Bell 3

MAP

The Ill Bell ridge, from Stile End

ASCENT FROM GARBURN PASS
1050 feet of ascent : 2½ miles

ILL BELL

2300
2200
2100

upper
Kentmere
Valley

old
quarry

YOKE

2200

stile
and gap

2000 2100

1900

1800
1700

Above the wall
there is no path
for 100 yards but
one will be found
higher up the slope

Rainsborrow
Crag

old
quarry

1600

quarry path

tarn

gate
sheep-pen

Troutbeck Valley

25 yards beyond the stream
a big cairn indicates the
indistinct turn to the
right from the main
path to the quarry.

1600

Buck
Crag

The variation start
from the pass, by the
wall, is very marshy.

Leave the pass at the point
where it turns sharply. The
first few yards are abominably
marshy. Aim for the small
cairns ahead.

1500

gate

KENTMERE
1½

gate

Garburn
Pass
1475'
(spelt Garbourn Pass
on Ordnance Survey maps)

TROUTBECK 2
WINDERMERE 4½

1400

looking north

This is the obvious route to Ill Bell, and
the only easy one. As far as Yoke it is a dull walk
although the dreary foreground is relieved by the
splendid views to the west. The route throughout
is on grass, in places marshy to the 1800' contour.

ASCENT FROM HAGG GILL, TROUTBECK
1700 feet of ascent

ASCENT FROM KENTMERE RESERVOIR
1500 feet of ascent

This is the second quarry in Hagg Gill (not the first) and a most interesting place it is. (The gates to it have to be climbed). Slant up to the left and ascend *beyond* the stream; a long featureless slope follows. *In mist the quarry is dangerous when descending*

looking north·east

Proceed to the head of the reservoir before turning up left to an obvious ridge. The rough upper slopes appear intimidating but steepness is the only difficulty. In wintry conditions this is a route for mountaineers only.

looking south·west

Ill Bell's continuously steep flanks are a challenge to those who prefer to reach their objective by rough scrambling, but walkers who walk for pleasure should take the easy promenade from the top of Garburn.

THE SUMMIT

The walker who toils up to the top of Ill Bell may be pardoned for feeling that he has achieved a major climb that has played a part of some consequence in mountaineering history, for he finds himself confronted by an imposing array of fine cairns that would do credit to a Matterhorn. And in fact this is a real mountain-top, small in extent and very rough; it is one of the most distinctive summits in Lakeland. There are some traces of the wire fence that used to follow the ridge.

DESCENTS: The Troutbeck flank is steep, the Kentmere side is *very* steep and rough. Neither is suitable for descent, nor is there need to attempt them, for all destinations south are much more easily reached by way of the ridge to Garburn Pass.

In mist, Garburn Pass *must* be the objective. Join a path in the depression south of the summit and when it becomes indistinct keep on to a wall that continues to the Pass.

The main cairn

N

FROSWICK

way to summit of

GARBURN PASS

YOKE

grass

× viewpoint
for Kentmere
Reservoir

2400

2300

50 YARDS

THE VIEW

Although higher fells northwards restrict the distant view in that direction, elsewhere it is good, the Scafells being prominent on the western skyline. Ill Bell is one of the classic 'stations' for viewing Windermere.

Principal Fells

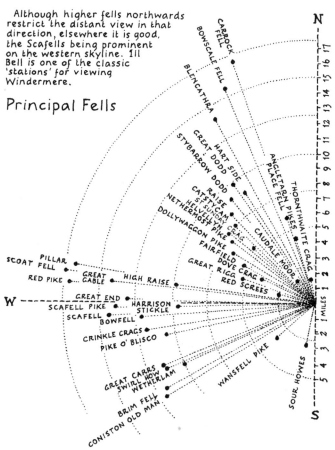

Lakes and Tarns

SSW : *Windermere*
SW : *Blelham Tarn*
NNW : A tiny strip of *Ullswater* is visible from the northern edge of the summit, 35 yards from main cairn.
E : *Kentmere Reservoir* is brought suddenly into view by walking 40 yards towards Harter Fell.

THE VIEW

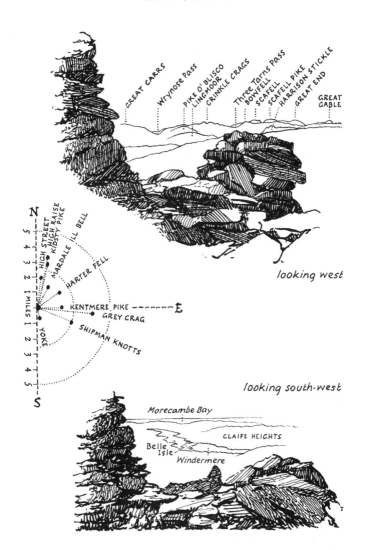

GREAT CARRS
Wrynose Pass
PIKE O' BLISCO
LINGMOOR
CRINKLE CRAGS
Three Tarns Pass
BOWFELL
SCAFELL
SCAFELL PIKE
HARRISON STICKLE
GREAT END
GREAT GABLE

looking west

N
S
E
MILES
5 4 3 2 1
1 2 3 4 5

HIGH STREET
KIDSTY PIKE
HIGH RAISE
MARDALE ILL BELL
HARTER FELL
KENTMERE PIKE
GREY CRAG
YOKE
SHIPMAN KNOTTS

looking south-west

Morecambe Bay
CLAIFE HEIGHTS
Belle Isle
Windermere

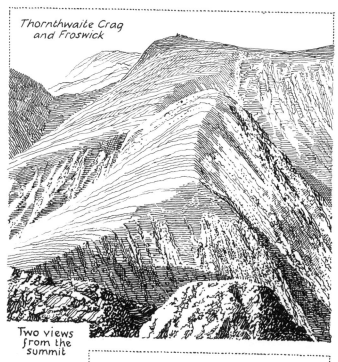

Thornthwaite Crag
and Froswick

Two views
from the
summit

Rainsborrow Cove
and Yoke

RIDGE ROUTES

To FROSWICK, 2359' : ⅔ mile : NW then N
Depression at 2075' : 285 feet of ascent
Rough at first, then easy walking

Turn west by the most northerly cairn, over stones (care needed in mist), and find a path going down north-west to the depression, beyond which is an easy climb on grass.

NOTE: The 1" Ordnance Survey map shows the height of the depression as *not less than 2100'*, the 2½" map as *not more than 2050'*. 2075' has been adopted here on the principle of moderation in all things.

ONE MILE

To YOKE, 2309' : ⅔ mile : S
Depression at 2180' : 130 feet of ascent
An easy walk, safe in mist

Descend by the southerly cairn. A faint track soon materialises and crosses the depression: at the far end, where it bifurcates, take the left branch along the edge of the escarpment. A wire fence is joined and leads over grass to the cairn. *In mist*, note that the cairn is adjacent to the *second* right-angle in the fence.

Ill Bell and the head of Kentmere

Kentmere Pike

2397'

HIGH
STREET ▲

Mardale Head

HARTER FELL ▲

ILL BELL ▲

KENTMERE
▲ PIKE ▲ TARN
CRAG

SHIPMAN KNOTTS ▲

● Kentmere

Longsleddale ●

MILES

0 1 2 3 4

from Ill Bell
(north-east ridge)

NATURAL FEATURES

A high ridge, a counterpart to the Ill Bell range across Kentmere, rises steeply to enclose the upper part of that valley on the east. This is the south ridge of Harter Fell, which, soon after leaving the parent summit, swells into the bare, rounded top of Kentmere Pike, a fell of some importance and of more significance to the inhabitants of the valley, as its name suggests, than Harter Fell itself. The Kentmere slope, wooded at its foot and craggy above, is of little interest, but the eastern flank is altogether of sterner stuff, falling precipitously into the narrow jaws of Longsleddale: a most impressive scene. Here, abrupt cliffs riven by deep gullies tower high above the crystal waters of the winding Sprint and give to the dalehead a savageness that contrasts strikingly with the placid sweetness of the Sadgill pastures just out of their shadow.

looking north-west

1 : The summit
2 : Shipman Knotts
3 : Ridge continuing to Harter Fell
4 : Goat Scar
5 : Steel Pike
6 : Steel Rigg
7 : Raven Crag
8 : Settle Earth
9 : Ullstone Gill
10 : River Kent
11 : Wren Gill
12 : River Sprint
13 : Sadgill Woods
14 : Kentmere
15 : Longsleddale

Steel Pike, from the quarry road

looking down a scree gully, eastern flank

MAP

ASCENT FROM KENTMERE
1900 feet of ascent : 3 miles

KENTMERE PIKE
Ordnance Survey column
2300
2200
grass
2100
2000
scree
peat hags
gap
Goat Scar
gully
1600
1800
1900
SHIPMAN KNOTTS
1500
grass
1700
small walled enclosure (ruins)
Withered Howe
gap
1400
1300
1200
scree
bracken
1100
boulder
1000
crag
ruins
gate
900
Hollowbank
Brockstones
signpost
plantation
LONGSLEDDALE 1½
(cart·track)
KENTMERE (road) 1

looking north

This ascent of Kentmere Pike's tame western flank gives no suspicion of the rugged nature of the eastern face that falls precipitously to Longsleddale. A simple detour to the cairn above Goat Scar (a fine viewpoint for the craggy fastnesses of Longsleddale) is very strongly recommended in clear weather.

A gate to the right of the cluster of buildings at Hollowbank gives access to the open fell. The path is indistinct initially, but develops into a definite groove, easily followed to the first wall. Beyond, the zig-zags are an interesting test in path-finding: here the path is not clear, but is worth searching for. It leads to the top wall — no gate or stile is provided in this, curiously — and a gap is used to reach the upper slopes of the fell.

The route shown is safe in mist.

A pleasant, well-graded climb along an old grooved path, with excellent views of Kentmere, although the last mile is dull. This is the easiest way onto the Harter Fell ridge.

ASCENT FROM LONGSLEDDALE
1850 feet of ascent : 3 miles from Sadgill

KENTMERE PIKE
Ordnance Survey column
→ HARTER FELL

The fence above the crags is in ruins, but sufficient still remains to form a safe guide to the summit-wall.

2300
2200
2100
2000
broken fence
1900
peat hags
Settle Earth
tarn
1800
1700

This walk should not be attempted in mist.

Goat Scar

Raven Crag

Steel Pike

Steel Rigg
1400
grass
1300
fall

scree
1200
1100
1000

rocky gorge pools and waterfalls

The Sprint cannot be forded at the junction of the wall running up the fell. Cross 50 yards lower. Note the profuse sheep-traces by the wall!

900
800
fold

During the steep ascent by the wall, Buckbarrow Crag gives ample excuse for halts : it is an imposing object just across the valley.

stile (giving access to Buckbarrow Crag)

Detours from the old fence to the edge of the cliffs may be made at several places; notably this should be done near the bend in the fence above Settle Earth.

fold
River Sprint
gravel flats
(a feature uncommon in Lakeland)
fold

looking north-west

quarry road

SADGILL ½

This is a savage scene but not all is desolation: the gorge of the Sprint is very beautiful, and there is a delightful, small, rock-girt tarn alongside the old fence.

This route has been devised for walkers who have a liking for impressive rock-scenery —— it is the only practicable way up the rough eastern face, and it affords striking views of the crags, first from below then in profile and lastly from above.

THE SUMMIT

The top of the fell, an unattractive and uninteresting place, is robbed of any appeal it might otherwise have had by a high wall that bisects it from end to end. A triangulation station of the Ordnance Survey in the form of a short column stands in the shelter of the east side of the wall, on a small rise, but its claim to occupy the highest point is disputed by a tiny pile of stones a few yards distant on the west side.

DESCENTS : To Kentmere : Anyone familiar with the grooved path going down to Hollowbank will have no difficulty in finding the start of it, at a break in the lower wall; strangers may not easily locate the gap and should instead continue by the ridge over Shipman Knotts to the Sadgill-Kentmere cart-track: *in mist, this route is safest.* For Longsleddale, too, it is best to make this cart-track the objective. *Much of the Longsleddale flank is craggy and dangerous,* although the route described as an ascent on page 6 is a safe way off in clear weather.

The eastern face, with Harter Fell beyond, from Goat Scar

THE VIEW

The distant view of Lakeland is interrupted by the nearer heights across Kentmere; it is interesting to note that the summit-cone of Ill Bell exactly conceals Scafell Pike. More satisfactory prospects are south-east, towards the Pennines, and south-west, over Windermere to Morecambe Bay.

Principal Fells

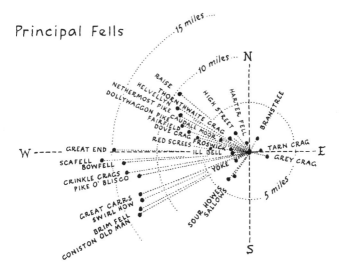

Lakes and Tarns
SSW : *Windermere*

Kentmere Reservoir is brought into view by walking 50 yards in the direction of Ill Bell.

RIDGE ROUTES

To HARTER FELL, 2539': 1¼ miles
NNW then N

Depression at 2275': 275 feet of ascent
Easy walking on grass; safe in mist

Walls at first and then broken fences link
the two summits (traces of the old fence on
the broad top of Harter Fell are scarce) and
indicate the route; intermittent path.

To SHIPMAN KNOTTS, 1926'
1¼ miles: SE then S

Depression at 1875': 80 feet of ascent
Easy walking, safe in mist

Continuous walls and fences link the summits
but, in clear weather, a short detour (100 yards)
should be made to the cairn on Goat Scar — an
excellent viewpoint for Longsleddale. A scree
gully and a steep crag distinguish the depression.

Branstree and the head of Longsleddale, from Goat Scar

Goat Scar
from
Longsleddale

Kidsty Pike

2560'

Patterdale

Hartsop ▲ HIGH RAISE
RAMPSGILL HEAD
▲ KIDSTY PIKE

Riggindale
▲ HIGH STREET

MILES
0 1 2 3 4

from Twopenny Crag

NATURAL FEATURES

Travellers on the road and railway at Shap, looking west to the long undulating skyline of the High Street range, will find their attention focussing on the most prominent feature there, the sharp peak of Kidsty Pike. This distinctive summit, which unmistakably identifies the fell whenever it is seen in profile, is formed by the sudden breaking of the gently-rising eastern slope in a precipice of crags and scree that falls very abruptly into the depths of Riggindale. The summit is the best feature of the fell. The Riggindale face is everywhere steep, but other slopes are easy except for an extensive area of rock halfway down the long eastern shoulder.

It is interesting to note that the raising of the level of Haweswater gave Kidsty Pike a 'footing' on the shore of the lake, for the first time — previously the confining becks of Randale and Riggindale united before reaching the lake, but now each enters as a separate feeder and the small strip of shore between is the new terminus of the fell.

The summit crags

MAP

ONE MILE

ASCENT FROM MARDALE

1900 feet of ascent : 3 miles from the road end

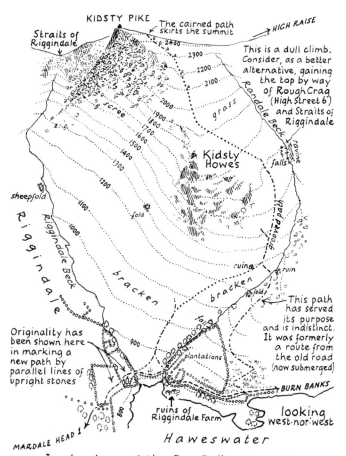

KIDSTY PIKE

The cairned path skirts the summit

HIGH RAISE

Straits of Riggindale

2400
2300
2200
2100
2000
1900
1800
1700
1600
1500
1400
1300
1200
1100
1000

scree

grass

Randale Beck

This is a dull climb. Consider, as a better alternative, gaining the top by way of Rough Crag (High Street 6) and Straits of Riggindale

Kidsty Howes

ravine

falls

grooved path

sheepfold

Riggindale Beck

fold

900

800

600

ruin

ruin

fold

Riggindale

bracken

bracken

This path has served its purpose and is indistinct. It was formerly a route from the old road (now submerged)

Originality has been shown here in marking a new path by parallel lines of upright stones

fall

plantations

BURN BANKS

ruins of Riggindale Farm

looking west-nor-west

MARDALE HEAD 1

Haweswater

In the days of the Dun Bull at Mardale Green this was a favourite ascent. Now it is rarely used: the paths have gone to seed, and tough grass makes the climb laborious. The easiest route is that shown.

THE SUMMIT

CAUDALE MOOR
CONISTON OLD MAN
BRIM FELL
RED SCREES
SWIRL HOW
GREAT CARRS
HARTER FELL
CRINKLE CRAGS

GRAY CRAG

Straits of
Riggindale

The summit is an eyrie perched high above Riggindale. The small cairn stands on grass amongst the boulders of the top pedestal, and crags are immediately below. The situation is dramatic. A narrow track leads to it from the north-west.

DESCENTS: For Patterdale or Hartsop, make a bee-line over Rampsgill Head, crossing it near the old signpost, and join the path below the Knott. For Mardale (if accommodation has been reserved) walk north to join a cairned track skirting the summit. Obviously there is no direct way into Riggindale. *In mist,* keep to the Straits of Riggindale track if bound for Patterdale or Hartsop, the path for which is joined near a wall. For Mardale, when the cairned track peters out bear half-left and descend with the music of Randale Beck kept a furlong away on the left hand to avoid ravines.

RIDGE ROUTE

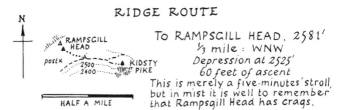

N

RAMPSGILL HEAD

post x

2500
2400

KIDSTY PIKE

HALF A MILE

To RAMPSGILL HEAD, 2581'
⅓ mile : WNW
Depression at 2525'
60 feet of ascent
This is merely a five-minutes' stroll, but in mist it is well to remember that Rampsgill Head has crags.

THE VIEW

The bulky masses of High Street, Rampsgill Head and High Raise, all in close proximity, cut out big slices of the distant panorama; but in those directions where the view is unrestricted, it is good.

Principal Fells

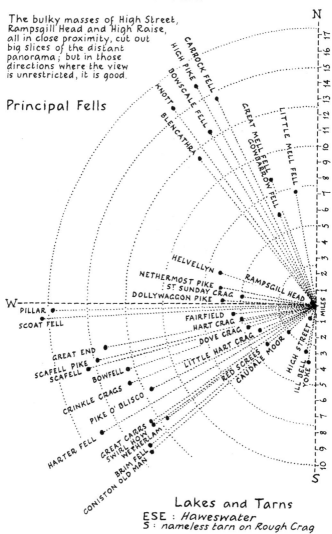

N

17 16 15 14 13 12 11 10 9 8 7 6 5 4 3 2 1 MILES

CARROCK FELL
HIGH PIKE
BOWSCALE FELL
KNOTT
BLENCATHRA
GREAT MELL FELL
GOWBARROW FELL
LITTLE MELL FELL

W

HELVELLYN
NETHERMOST PIKE
ST SUNDAY CRAG
DOLLYWAGGON PIKE
RAMPSGILL HEAD

PILLAR
SCOAT FELL
FAIRFIELD
HART CRAG
DOVE CRAG
LITTLE HART CRAG
GREAT END
SCAFELL PIKE
SCAFELL
BOWFELL
CRINKLE CRAGS
PIKE O' BLISCO
RED SCREES
CAUDALE MOOR
HIGH STREET
ILL BELL
YOKE

HARTER FELL
GREAT CARRS
SWIRL HOWE
WETHERLAM
BRIM FELL
CONISTON OLD MAN

S

Lakes and Tarns

ESE : *Haweswater*
S : *nameless tarn on Rough Crag*

THE VIEW

High Street

Selside Pike and Haweswater

The Knott

2423'

Patterdale

Hartsop ▲ HIGH RAISE

▲ ▲ RAMPSGILL HEAD
THE KNOTT

▲ HIGH STREET

MILES

0   1   2   3   4

from Hayeswater Gill

NATURAL FEATURES

The steep western slope descending from Rampsgill Head is arrested below the summit, just as the fall is gathering impetus, by a protuberance that takes the shape of a small conical hill. This is the Knott, a key point for walkers in this area, and although its short side rises barely a hundred feet from the main fell, its appearance is imposing when seen from other directions and especially when approached from the Hartsop valley. Fans of scree litter its western flank, which goes down steeply to Hayeswater; a tremendous scree gully here is the Knott's one interesting feature.

MAP

ONE MILE

N

PATTERDALE 3

REST DODD

1900 2000

1700

1600

1500

1400

1300

sulphury Gill

gate

gate

HARTSOP 1

gates

1400

dam

sheep pen

THE KNOTT 2423'

Rampsgill

continuation RAMPSGILL HEAD 4

2400

2500

GRAY CRAG

Hayeswater

moraines

gully

1500 1700 1800 1900 2000 2100 2200 2300

1600

1400

Straits of Riggindale

gate

gate

Note that the scale of this map is larger than that commonly used in this book

continuation GRAY CRAG 2

continuation HIGH STREET 4

ASCENT FROM HARTSOP
1850 feet of ascent : 2 miles

THE KNOTT

REST DODD

HIGH STREET

S C R E E

Scree Gully

scree

peat-hags

gate

2300
2200
2100 scree
2000
1900
1800
1700

PATTERDALE 3

GRAY CRAG

sheep-pen

1700

Sulphury Gill descends in a series of cascades

1600

1500

Sulphury Gill

1400 1300

Prison Gill

gates

dam

Hayeswater

ford

cascades

The rickety footbridge over the stile near the filter house is (at the time of writing) unexpectedly safe
STOP PRESS! —
New bridge. 1956

BROCK CRAGS

gate stile

filter house

1300
1200

1100
gate
1000

barn

Wath Bridge

Pasture Beck

THRESHTHWAITE MOUTH

gate

1200
1100
1000
900

ruin
gate
ruin

Incidentally, this route is the quickest way to the High Street from the Kirkstone road

Normally the path on the right side of the gill from Wath Bridge is best, but if the beck is in spate the ford may be impassable and it is then advisable to keep on the left side of the gill past the filter house

800

Hayeswater Gill

gate

Walker Bridge

Low Hartsop

looking east

As far as Hayeswater, this is a fine approach; beyond, it deteriorates into a dull trudge.

THE SUMMIT

HIGH RAISE   RAMPSGILL HEAD

The small top of the fell is without interest except for some bouldery excavations overlooking the gully on the south which seem artificial. A wall crosses the summit, forming an angle; a few paces away is the cairn. **DESCENTS**: Follow the wall either way to join the path.

THE VIEW

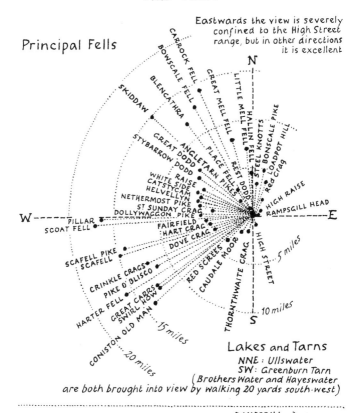

Principal Fells

Eastwards the view is severely confined to the High Street range, but in other directions it is excellent

Labels (clockwise from N): CARROCK FELL, BOWSCALE FELL, BLENCATHRA, GREAT MELL FELL, LITTLE MELL FELL, HALLIN FELL, STEEL KNOTTS, BONSCALE PIKE, LOADPOT HILL, Red Crag, HIGH RAISE, RAMPSGILL HEAD, SKIDDAW, STYBARROW DODD, GREAT DODD, ANGLETARN PIKES, PLACE FELL, REST DODD, WHITE SIDE, RAISE, CATSTYCAM, HELVELLYN, NETHERMOST PIKE, ST SUNDAY CRAG, DOLLYWAGGON PIKE, FAIRFIELD, HART CRAG, DOVE CRAG, PILLAR, SCOAT FELL, SCAFELL PIKE, SCAFELL, CRINKLE CRAGS, PIKE O'BLISCO, HARTER FELL, GREAT CARRS, SWIRL HOW, CONISTON OLD MAN, RED SCREES, CAUDALE MOOR, THORNTHWAITE CRAG, HIGH STREET

N, W, E, S

5 miles, 10 miles, 15 miles, 20 miles

Lakes and Tarns
NNE: Ullswater
SW: Greenburn Tarn
(Brothers Water and Hayeswater are both brought into view by walking 20 yards south-west)

RIDGE ROUTES

To RAMPSGILL HEAD, 2581′: ⅓ mile: E
Depression at 2360′: 225 feet of ascent
An easy climb. Avoid cliffs (on left) in mist

To REST DODD, 2278′: ¾ mile: NNW
Depression at 1925′: 360 feet of ascent
A straightforward walk, following the wall until it turns left, then directly ahead to the top

RAMPSGILL HEAD, 2500, 2400, THE KNOTT, 2300, 2100, 2000, gate, REST DODD, N, QUARTER MILE

Loadpot Hill

2201'

from Sandwick

• Pooley Bridge
Askham•
Helton •
▲ ARTHUR'S PIKE
• Howtown
LOADPOT
▲ HILL
Bampton•
▲ WETHER HILL

MILES
0 1 2 3 4

The Beacon on The Pen

NATURAL FEATURES

The High Street range, narrow-waisted at the impressive Straits of Riggindale, thereafter develops buxom girth as it proceeds north. Although the western flank continues steep to its extremity on Arthur's Pike, the eastern slopes descend gradually and irresolutely, halting often in wide plateaux and covering a considerable tract of moorland that is intersected by a succession of deep-cut gills, all of which join the main lateral valley of Mardale and the River Lowther. Nowhere is this characteristic manifest more than in Loadpot Hill, and because Loadpot Hill is the last of the principal eminences of the range it also has northern slopes, no less extensive, which exhibit the same reluctance to depart from the high places: hence the gradients are easy, with subsidiary hillocks arresting the decline. By Lakeland standards (which demand at least a glimpse of *rock* in every scene) territory of this type is uninteresting, for all hereabouts is tough grass and heather except for the single shattered scree-rash of Brock Crag, above Fusedale; yet there is a haunting attractiveness about these far-flung rolling expanses. There is the appearance of desolation, but no place is desolate that harbours so much life: in addition to the inevitable sheep, hardy fell ponies roam and graze at will, summer and winter alike, and the Martindale deer often cross the watershed; in springtime especially, the number and variety of birds is quite unusual for the fells. There is little to disturb these creatures. Man is not the enemy, only the fox and the buzzard. Loadpot Hill is a natural sanctuary for all wild life.

1 : The summit
2 : Arthur's Pike
3 : Bonscale Pike
4 : Brock Crag
5 : The Pen
6 : Brown Rigg
7 : Moor Divock

8 : River Lowther
9 : Cawdale Beck
10 : Heltondale Beck
11 : Aik Beck

12 : Swarthbeck Gill
13 : Fusedale Beck
14 : Ullswater

looking south

Cop Stone
and an oddly-sited
signpost

The antiquities
and oddities of
Moor Divock

Tumuli

Man may (and does) neglect Loadpot Hill nowadays, but it was not always so. There are evidences in plenty of the esteem with which it has been regarded in the past. Even before the Romans traversed it with their High Street, its slopes were the home and meeting-place of man. There is a stone circle created by human agency near the headwaters of Swarthbeck Gill, Druidical remains and other curiosities in surprising profusion on Moor Divock on the 1050' contour, while, nearer our own time, men have laboured to erect an elaborate system of parochial boundary stones and posts along Loadpot's top and down its flanks. (It is a contrasting commentary on a modern enlightened age that the most recent erections on the Moor are shooting-hides from which the harmless and helpless grouse may be killed and crippled). And no other Lakeland fell has a domestic chimney-stack and a concrete living-room floor almost on its summit!

A boundary stone

A boundary post

Moor Divock is of very special interest to the antiquarian and archæologist, and has long been a happy hunting-ground for them. The geologist will be concerned with investigating the crater-like hollows or sinkholes (locally known as swallows), which incidentally often contain carcasses and skeletons. The humbler pedestrian, not versed in the sciences, will be impressed by the spaciousness and loneliness of the scene and the excellence of its principal path.

Stone Circles

MAP

Loadpot Hill is the principal eminence of the High Street range at the northern extremity, and is extensive in area. Five pages of maps are necessary in order to show fully the main approaches to the fell from the villages at its base.

MAP

Reference should be made to the note at the top of page 8 before this map is consulted.

continuation LOADPOT HILL 7

ONE MILE

MAP

Reference should be made to the note at the top
of page 8 before this map is consulted.

continuation LOADPOT HILL 8

ONE MILE

MAP

Reference should be made to the note at the top of page 8 before this map is consulted.

If the ascent is commenced from Pooley Bridge, a visit to Arthur's Pike should be considered: such a detour *en route* entails little extra time, is a pleasanter way to the tops, and is more rewarding in Ullswater views. If this course is followed, a beeline (no path) from the gate at Roehead to the top corner of the plantation wall may be made (but during or after rain there will be boggy patches and then the recognised paths will provide drier walking-routes)

continuation LOADPOT HILL 5

MAP

NOTE on the Loadpot Hill maps:

Walkers bound for the summit, especially from the north and east, may have difficulty in finding access to the fell: routes cannot be determined by observation from valley-level because of intervening tracts of cultivated farmland, which must be traversed before open ground is reached. A maze of byways and walled enclosures and farmsteads complicates the approaches. Many variations may be made, but the accompanying maps illustrate only the most direct routes, and, to depict them more clearly, *much unnecessary detail in the cultivated areas has been omitted.*

Those walkers who, like the author, do not enjoy encounters with cows and young bulls and the sundry other mammals that commonly frequent confined farmyards will be relieved to learn that the routes illustrated have been specially selected to reduce this possibility to a minimum, and only at one place (Carhullan) is it necessary to pass through a farmyard.

PENRITH 4½

LOWTHER 1½

Askham

gate

cart track

gate

Whitbysteads

old quarry

continuation opposite

1000

Stone Circle

Heltonhead

signpost

Cop Stone

tarmac road (unenclosed)

sinkholes

gate

Widewath

Helton

gate

N

ONE MILE

ASCENTS FROM BAMPTON AND HELTON
1650 feet of ascent
4½ miles from Bampton ; 5½ miles from Helton

LOADPOT HILL

WETHER HILL

chimney

grass — 2100

groove — 2000

wall — 1900

— 1800

sheep fold

grass

MOOR DIVOCK

— 1800

— 1700

— 1600

— 1500

— 1400

— 1300

— 1200

— 1100

Black fell ponies graze on the upper slopes. They are docile

Cawdale Beck

The Pen

beacon

Inkern Beck

heather

heather

Heltondale Beck

Cawdale

quarry

Pen End

There is one breach in the cultivated land where the moor comes down almost to the road: the Helton route traverses this

Carhullan 1100

Moorahill

High Howe

gate

Rough Hill Tarn

unenclosed tarmac road

rough pasture

gate

1000

Roughill Tarn Gate postbox

Sceugh

tarmac road

rough pasture

Lanty Crag

tarmac road

MOOR DIVOCK

Low Hullockhowe

900

800

gate

cultivated farmland

700

700

barn

HELTON

footbridge

Beckfoot

gate

Hows Beck

waterfall

quarry

gate

The first field on the approach from Bampton — a common — has many charming waterfalls, and more rock than will be met on the whole of the rest of the walk

Beckfoot Bridge

½

Bampton

looking west

The Helton route is rather the more interesting of the two illustrated, but both are pleasant walks in quiet, unexciting surroundings. The upper slopes are simple and very easy, but deceptively long.

ASCENT FROM MOOR DIVOCK
1300 feet of ascent : 4½ miles

Full route from POOLEY BRIDGE
1800 feet of ascent : 6 miles

Full route from ASKHAM
1600 feet of ascent : 6½ miles

LOADPOT HILL

(chimney on south side)

grass △ 2100

2000 Loadpot Hole

Fell ponies are likely to be seen on these slopes where they live all the year. When the fell is under deep snow they are fed from the farms. Many go to work in the coal-pits.

groove

1900 grass

boundary stone ×

rutted path

○○ Standing Stones (only one remains standing — and *that* one leans badly)

The gradients are everywhere simple. Even the most decrepit hiker will surmount them with ease.

Bridge in Heltondale

HIGH STREET (ROMAN ROAD)

1800

Swarthbeck Gill

1700 × reservoirs

sheepfold

ARTHUR'S PIKE

beacon

All the reservoirs shown on this diagram are covered. But not Jeannie's delectable chalice!

Jeannie Brewster's Well ○

grass

× boundary stone

× reservoirs 1600

× reservoir

grass path in heather

White Knott

Heltondale

shooting box ○

1000

gorse

1200 1300 1100

1400 1500

heather

Brown Rigg

× reservoir

reservoir

HOWTOWN

bracken

HELTON

tarmac road (unenclosed)

bridge

heather

signpost

Cop Stone ○

Aik Beck

faint track

shooting butt

ravine

This is positively the worst bog on any regular Lakeland path. Avoid it!

Wolf Holes

Stone Circle ○○○

sinkholes

Pulpit Holes

1100

Moor Divock

○ bog

tumuli

Stone Circle

The place to turn off the Howtown path is NOT distinct. Do this 300 yards beyond the Circle

bracken

stone post (boundary)

good wide path

△ cairn

wide path

Elder Beck

ASKHAM

bracken

POOLEY BRIDGE

looking south-south-west

This is not a walk for a wet or misty day, and ample time should be allowed. The High Street of the Romans is now, at best, only a line of ruts in the grass. The ascent *via* Arthur's Pike is recommended for its superior views.

ASCENT FROM HOWTOWN
1750 feet of ascent : 2¼ miles

LOADPOT HILL

HIGH RAISE

chimney

BAMPTON

2100

Loadpot
Hole

2000

WETHER HILL

HIGH STREET
(ROMAN ROAD)

1900

MOOR DIVOCK

1800

small
tarns

1700

1600

1800

Standing Stones
(only one now
remains standing)

Brock
Crag

1500

1400

1300

1200 1000

1800

In late summer
tall bracken
impedes
progress
here

WETHER HILL

BONSCALE
PIKE

1600

Dodd Gill

scree gully

900

Fusedale Beck

FUSEDALE

BONSCALE PIKE

scree

1300

1200

800

700

Cote

bracken

1000

gate

Mellguards

cart track

The approach
to Loadpot Hill
from Howtown is
the shortest and far
the best, the dullness of
the climb being relieved by
the beautiful retrospect
over Martindale

MOOR DIVOCK

500

gate

gate

looking
south-east

Howtown Hotel

Fusedale and
Ullswater
from Dodd Gill

Brock Crag
and Ullswater

THE SUMMIT

Reference has already been made to the attention paid to Loadpot Hill since ancient times, and this is also manifest in the cairn on the summit — somebody, sometime, has gone to the trouble to collect, somewhere, a number of handsome stones foreign to the immediate neighbourhood, all prominently displaying a glittering quartz content, and transport them, somehow, to the highest point; these form a cairn around the base of a boundary-stone, which itself bears the inscriptions of a benchmark (�) and a capital letter L (probably for Lowther).

Apart from this cairn, and another adorned with a flagstaff, the summit is unremarkable. All is grass and all is flat, and more like a 30-acre field than a mountain top.

DESCENTS: Descents may be made easily and safely in any direction. (Loadpot *Hole* is not a hazard to avoid — it is not a hole one can fall into but a shallow landslip, which, because it faces north, holds the last snow on the fell every spring).

In mist, the walker should not be here at all, but if he is his best plan is probably to descend westwards to the High Street (only a rut in the grass) and follow it to Moor Divock: not an easy task. *If conditions are bad* cross High Street and, still heading west, go down the steepening bracken slopes into Fusedale (for Howtown)

Just below and south of the summit is the one landmark that distinguishes this fell from all others. This is the chimney of Lowther House, a former shooting-lodge, with stables: the wooden structure has now been dismantled and taken away, but the stone stack of the chimney, now an ornament of no use, still points forlornly to the sky.

Chimney, Lowther House

THE VIEW

Principal Fells

One half of the panorama is Lakeland, dominated by the high, imposing range of Helvellyn; the other half is Pennine, with Cross Fell and its satellites prominent

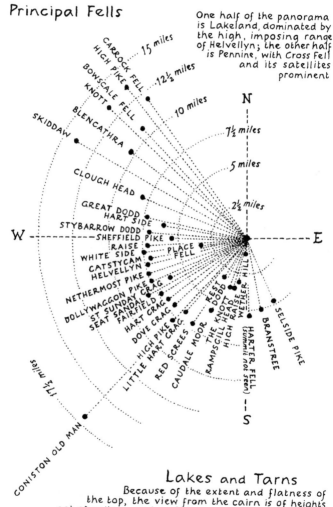

CARROCK FELL
HIGH PIKE
15 miles
BOWSCALE FELL
12½ miles
KNOTT
10 miles
SKIDDAW
BLENCATHRA
7½ miles
N
5 miles
CLOUGH HEAD
2½ miles
GREAT DODD
HART SIDE
STYBARROW DODD
SHEFFIELD PIKE
W
RAISE
PLACE FELL
E
WHITE SIDE
CATSTYCAM
HELVELLYN
NETHERMOST PIKE
DOLLYWAGGON PIKE
ST SUNDAY CRAG
SEAT SANDAL CRAG
FAIRFIELD
REST DODD
HART CRAG
THE KNOTT
DOVE CRAG
HIGH RAISE
WETHER HILL
HIGH PIKE
RAMPSGILL HEAD
SELSIDE PIKE
LITTLE HART CRAG
RED SCREES
CAUDALE MOOR
HARTER FELL (summit not seen)
BRANSTREE
S
17½ miles
CONISTON OLD MAN

Lakes and Tarns

Because of the extent and flatness of the top, the view from the cairn is of heights, not of valleys, and no lakes are visible. Ullswater, however, can be seen by walking 150 yards towards the west

RIDGE ROUTES

To ARTHUR'S PIKE, 1747': 2¼ miles
NW, then NNE and N

Minor depressions: 50 feet of ascent
An easy walk, not recommended in mist

Descend the easy western slope to the
High Street and follow it over the first
rise, where trend left (no path)
to the summit directly ahead,
crossing a fair path
en route. Visit the
ruined beacon for the
best view of Ullswater.

To BONSCALE PIKE, 1718'
1½ miles: NW, then N

Minor depressions:
50 feet of ascent
An easy walk, not safe in mist

Descend the easy western slope
to the High Street, but at the
angle of the path leave it
and continue north over
sundry grassy mounds (no
path) to the inconspicuous
cairn above a fringe of crag
where stand two prominent
pillars, the *lower* of the two
being Bonscale Tower.

To WETHER HILL, 2210'
1 mile: S

Depression at 2025'
200 feet of ascent

An easy walk, safe in mist

The High Street inclined to the left
below Lowther House, but has become
indistinct and is now badly cut about
by peat-hags in the depression. Easier
walking is found on a new path, not yet
quite easy to follow, which crosses the
depression on its right (i.e. west) side,
away from the hags. There should be
no difficulty in mist: all gradients
are easy — if steep ground is
encountered the route is lost.

Mardale Ill Bell

2496'

from the north ridge of
Branstree

HIGH STREET
▲

Mardale
● Head

MARDALE
ILL BELL
▲

▲ HARTER FELL

▲ ILL BELL

● Kentmere

MILES
0   1   2   3   4

NATURAL FEATURES

Mardale Ill Bell has received scant mention in Lakeland literature, and admittedly is mainly of nondescript appearance, yet one aspect of the fell is particularly good and appeals on sight to all who aspire to a little mild mountaineering. This is to the north-east, where a boulder-strewn shoulder leaves the summit and soon divides into two craggy ridges, enclosing a rocky corrie; the rugged surroundings on this side are greatly enhanced in impressiveness by the two splendid tarns of Blea Water (below High Street) and Small Water (below Harter Fell), each of them occupying a volcanic crater and deeply inurned amongst crags. These tarns, with their streams, are collectively known as Mardale Waters, and greatly contribute to the fine scenic quality of this typical Lakeland landscape.

To the west the fell merges gently and dully into High Street, with a fringe of crag throughout on the north; and south of the linking high ground is a wall of steep rock, Bleathwaite Crag, bounding the silent hollow of Hall Cove, the birthplace of the River Kent. On the south also is the most pronounced shoulder of the fell, Lingmell End, thrusting far into the valley of Kentmere, and from it descends a short spur to the top of Nan Bield Pass.

looking north-west

1 : The summit   2 : Lingmell End
3 : Ridge continuing to High Street
4 : Nan Bield Pass   5 : Piot Crag   6 : North ridge
7 : East ridge   8 : Blea Water   9 : Small Water
10 : Blea Water Beck   11 : Small Water Beck
12 : Dodderwick Force   13 : River Kent   14 : Lingmell Gill

Waterfalls,
River Kent
below Hall Cove

Dodderwick
Force

The north face
from Blea Water

MAP

ASCENT FROM MARDALE
1700 feet of ascent : 2 miles from the road end

A: East ridge
B: North ridge

The east ridge is most easily attained by the grass slope from Small Water (just before the shelters are reached).

The north ridge is best attained from the outlet (small dam) of Blea Water, avoiding the path from the sheepfold. The rock rib is an easy scramble.

The orthodox route of ascent (and the best for descent) is via Nan Bield Pass.

looking west·south·west

Of the many excellent climbs available from Mardale Head the direct ascent of Mardale Ill Bell ranks high, the walk being favoured by striking views of two of the finest tarns in Lakeland, each set amongst crags in wild and romantic surroundings.

ASCENT FROM KENTMERE
2100 feet of ascent : 4¾ miles

← HIGH STREET

MARDALE ILL BELL

In descending to Nan Bield from the summit *in mist* — note that the pass is in the *second depression along the ridge, not the first.*

Nan Bield Pass

Hall Cove

Lingmell End

grass

scree

scree

scree

← These zig-zags are delightful

2300 2400 2200 2200 2100 2000 1900 1800 1700 1600 1500 1400 1300 1200 1100 1000

The climb up Lingmell End is easy, but steep, needing the use of hands. *This is not a route for descent in mist.*

sheepfold

Lingmell Gill

grass

cairned path

grass

River Kent

HALL COVE

bracken

This is the usual Kentmere route to Nan Bield (for details of the start see Harter Fell 6)

Smallthwaite Knott

1500
1400
1300

Kentmere Reservoir

bracken

Lingmell Gill now debouches into the reservoir through a breach in the bank but was originally diverted to run alongside and join the outflow.

fold

ford

1200

1100

1000

900

quarries

The Tongue

grass

KENTMERE via Overend 3

Kentmere Quarries

gate

KENTMERE via Hartrigg 2½

looking north

This is a dull climb but affords a good introduction to the fine Kentmere valley-head. Nan Bield is the best feature.

THE SUMMIT

Haweswater

Haweswater

Two cairns, forty yards apart, crown the north-east corner of the undulating top, which is characterised by soft turf, patches of brown stones and occasional outcrops. There is nothing here to suggest the presence of fine crags close by, and a visit to them (north) adds interest to the summit.

DESCENTS: The usual way off is via Nan Bield Pass (the wall-shelter on the top of the pass is plainly visible from the summit-cairn); to reach it, keep to the right of the direct line until a cairned path materialises. Both the north and east ridges are rough and the Lingmell End route is steep.

▌ *In mist, aim for Nan Bield Pass, noting that it crosses the second depression reached, not the first.*

grass

HIGH STREET

grass

NORTH EAST RIDGES

quartz boulders

LINGMELL END

NAN BIELD PASS

N

2400...

100 yards

The stone shelters at Small Water

THE VIEW

Outstanding in the moderate view is the neighbouring ridge of Ill Bell, which, displaying its steep and rugged eastern face, looks magnificent from this angle. The long curve of High Street hides most of the western fells, and only the tips of the Bowfell group are visible above the rising skyline of Thornthwaite Crag.

Principal Fells

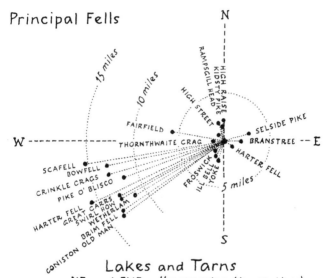

Lakes and Tarns

NE and ENE: Haweswater (two sections)

Neither *Blea Water* nor *Small Water* can be seen from the cairn but both are worth the detour necessary to obtain bird's-eye views of them, the former from a break in the crags 100 yards north, the latter from above Piot Crag a quarter of a mile due east.

The stone shelters at Small Water (illustration opposite)

Testimony to the former importance of Nan Bield Pass as a route for travellers and trade are the three shelters alongside the track where it crosses the bouldery shore of Small Water — erected for wayfarers overtaken by bad weather or darkness. These shelters are roughly but soundly built and roofed, but they are low and can be entered only by crawling. Once the body is insinuated snugly in their spider-infested recesses, however, the weather may be defied.

RIDGE ROUTES

To HIGH STREET, 2718′ : ⁴⁄₅ mile : WNW then NW
Depression at 2350′ : 400 feet of ascent
An easy walk with interesting views

A sketchy path leaves the summit but is of little consequence; it is preferable to follow the edge of the escarpment after crossing the depression. At one point, marked by a cairn, there is a sensational downward view of Blea Water. In mist, incline west to the wall.

To THORNTHWAITE CRAG, 2569′
1⅓ miles : WNW, then WSW, W & NW
Depressions at 2350′ and 2475′
250 feet of ascent

Easy walking, confusing in mist. When the short turf gives place to rough grass, keep the rising slope on the right hand and climb very slightly (*do not descend to left*). A track will be found as the end of the wall comes into sight.

To HARTER FELL, 2539′ : 1 mile : SE. then ESE and E
Depression at 2100′ (Nan Bield Pass) : 500 feet of ascent
A rough but interesting walk, with beautiful and impressive views

Aim first for the top of Nan Bield Pass (the wall-shelter there is in view from the summit), keeping to the right of the direct line until a cairned path to it is reached. Beyond the pass, an interesting ridge rises in rocky steps to the flat top of Harter Fell. In mist, the main difficulty will be in locating the Pass

*Haweswater and Small Water
from the Nan Bield ridge*

The summit crags

The Nab

from Rampsgill Beck

The Nab is situated wholly within
the Martindale Deer Forest. The
boundaries of the Forest are
principally defined by the
'Forest Wall', which encloses
much of the Rampsgill and
Bannerdale valleys and
crosses the high ground
between. This wall does
not confine the deer —
they roam freely beyond
the boundaries — but it
marks their home, their
only safe refuge, their one
sanctuary.
PLEASE DO NOT INTRUDE.

Red Deer
Stag

NATURAL FEATURES

The Nab is, in character, akin to the three Dodds around Kirkstonefoot. Very steep-sided, soaring in symmetrical lines to a slender cone, it appears from the pastures of Martindale as a lofty wedge splitting the valley into two branches, Rampsgill and Bannerdale: from this viewpoint it may well be thought to be a separate and solitary fell. But in fact, as is seen from neighbouring heights, it is merely the butt of the northern shoulder of Rest Dodd. Its lower slopes are of bracken, its higher reaches of grass, with occasional scree on both flanks and a few rocks on Nab End. In addition to its other distinctions it has, on the wide ridge behind the summit, a most unpleasant morass of peat-hags, one of the worst in the district.

MAP

The only public right-of-way on this map is the valley road from Dalehead

The 1" Ordnance Survey Map shows three paths on The Nab
— these are PRIVATE stalkers paths.

to MARTINDALE CHURCH 1¼

Dalehead

The Bungalow

Bannerdale

Bannerdale Beck

Rampsgill

Rampsgill Beck

gate

Nab End

THE NAB 1887

ONE MILE

N

Yewgrove Gill

falls

tarn

continuation REST DODD 2

ASCENTS

'Keep Out' notices, barricaded gates, and miles of barb wire must convey the impression even to the dullest-witted walker that there is no welcome here.   That impression is correct. Wandering within the boundaries of the Deer Forest is not encouraged.   Permission to visit the area should be sought at the keeper's Bungalow, and, justifiably, may not be granted.

The author carried out his explorations surreptitiously, and without permission (not caring to risk a refusal): he was not detected, but this may possibly have been due to his marked resemblance to an old stag, and other trespassers must not expect the same good fortune.   Walkers in general should keep away.   The keen 'peak-bagger' who is 'collecting' summits over 1886" must settle the matter with his conscience, and, if he decides he cannot omit The Nab, he may best approach it unobtrusively (but with permission) by way of the ridge from Rest Dodd, returning the same way.   The following notes on direct ascents will therefore be of little interest to anybody but deer with a poor sense of direction.

The natural route of ascent is from Martindale.
The three stalkers paths are distinct where they
have been cut into the fellside, but the
origins of the central and westerly
paths in the lower enclosure (to
which access is both barred and
barbed) have largely vanished.
The central route is most direct
although the path becomes clear
only beyond the gate in the cross-wall
at 1300', and it has the advantage (which
the others have not) that it continues, with
one sharp angle, to within a few paces of the summit-cairn.

THE SUMMIT

The summit, a shapely dome, is completely grassy. A few stones have been carried up and make an untidy cairn.

The top of the central path is found within twenty yards on the west side of the cairn. It leads first south-west, away from its destination.

THE VIEW

Principal Fells

The view is 'open' only to the north. The most interesting feature, however, is the snug fit of Scafell Pike in the frame of Deepdale Hause

CARROCK FELL
BOWSCALE FELL
KNOTT
BLENCATHRA
SKIDDAW
GREAT MELL FELL
GOWBARROW FELL
LITTLE MELL FELL
N
HALLIN FELL
BEDA FELL
STEEL KNOTTS
BONSCALE PIKE
LOADPOT HILL
WETHER HILL
10 miles
GREAT DODD
STYBARROW DODD
PLACE FELL
RAISE
WHITE SIDE
CATSTYCAM
HELVELLYN
NETHERMOST PIKE
ANGLETARN PIKES
St SUNDAY CRAG
FAIRFIELD
HART CRAG
DOVE CRAG
LITTLE HART CRAG
RED SCREES
CAUDALE MOOR
THE KNOTT
REST DODD (summit not seen)
HIGH STREET
RAMPSGILL HEAD
HIGH RAISE
15 miles
5 miles
W
E
SCAFELL PIKE
CONISTON OLD MAN
S

Lakes and Tarns
NNE: *Ullswater*

N

RIDGE ROUTE

To REST DODD, 2278': 1¼ miles
S, then W and SE
Depression at 1650': 650 feet of ascent
Avoid the worst of the peat-hags by keeping to the left edge of the depression, above Rampsgill, until firm ground is reached

▲ THE NAB
falls
peat hags
tarn
peat hags
HALF A MILE
1800
1700
1600
1500
1400
1300
1200
1100
1000
900
1700
1800
gate
2000
2100
2200
▲ REST DODD

Place Fell

2154'

from Birks

Howtown •

▲ PLACE FELL

• Patterdale

MILES
0   1   2   3

Few fells are so well favoured as Place Fell for appraising neighbouring heights.   It occupies an exceptionally good position in the curve of Ullswater, in the centre of a great bowl of hills; its summit commands a very beautiful and impressive panorama. On a first visit to Patterdale, Place Fell should be an early objective, for no other viewpoint gives such an appreciation of the design of this lovely corner of Lakeland.

NATURAL FEATURES

Place Fell rises steeply from the curve formed by the upper and middle reaches of Ullswater and its bulky mass dominates the head of the lake. Of only moderate elevation, and considerably overtopped by surrounding heights, nevertheless the fell more than holds its own even in such a goodly company: it has that distinctive blend of outline and rugged solidity characteristic of the true mountain. Many discoveries await those who explore: in particular the abrupt western flank, richly clothed with juniper and bracken and heather, and plunging down to the lake in a rough tumble of crag and scree, boulders and birches, is a paradise for the scrambler, while a more adventurous walker will find a keen enjoyment in tracing the many forgotten and overgrown paths across the fellside and in following the exciting and airy sheep-tracks that so skilfully contour the steep upper slopes below the hoary crest.

The eastern face, overlooking Boardale, is riven by deepcut gullies and is everywhere steep. Northward two ridges descend more gradually to the shores of Ullswater after passing over minor summits; from a lonely hollow between them issues the main stream on the fell, Scalehow Beck, which has good waterfalls. To the south, Boardale Hause is a well-known walkers' crossroads, and beyond this depression high ground continues to climb towards the principal watershed.

looking south

1 : The summit
2 : The Knight
3 : Birk Fell   4 : High Dodd
5 : Sleet Fell   6 : Mortar Crag   7 : Long Crag
8 : Goldrill Beck   9 : Scalehow Beck   10 : Scalehow Force   12 : Boardale
11 : Boardale Beck   13 : Patterdale   14 : Silver Point   15 : Ullswater

MAP

It is the author's opinion that the lakeside path from Scalehow Beck, near Sandwick, to Patterdale (in that direction) is the most beautiful and rewarding walk in Lakeland.
The junction of paths at Silver Bay is indistinct and easily missed. The higher (east) path branches off left 70 yards short of the beck running into the bay.

MAP

ONE MILE

On the 2½" and 6" Ordnance, and Bartholomew's maps Boardalehead is spelt 'Boredalehead'

PLAN OF LOW MOSS

The sheepfold on Low Moss is the Mecca of lost pilgrims on the extensive north-eastern slopes. Many paths converge hereabouts; all are indistinct.

1: to Sandwick via Scalehow. 2: to High Dodd
3: to Sandwick via Boardale 4: to Boardale
5: to Place Fell summit. 6 & 7: to The Knight

PLAN OF BOARDALE HAUSE

Boardale Hause is a walkers' crossroads and the maze of paths is confusing; but each has a definite objective. The Hause is crossed by the Hayeswater Aqueduct, and, to confound the traveller further, recent tractor trails during pipelaying operations have added new routes and obliterated portions of long-established paths.

1: to Patterdale. 2: to Place Fell
3: to Boardale. 4: to Martindale
5 & 6: to Angletarn Pikes

A.B: Inspection chambers
C.D.E: Air valves

The small ruined enclosure on the Hause (marked 'ruin' on the plan) is not an old sheepfold, as it appears to be, but the remains of a chapel; a few carved stones still lie about. The large-scale Ordnance maps name it 'Chapel in the Hause'.

ASCENT FROM PATTERDALE
1700 feet of ascent : 1¾ miles

The face of Place Fell overlooking Patterdale is unremittingly and uncompromisingly steep, and the ascent is invariably made by way of the easier gradients of Boardale Hause, there being a continuous path on this route. (*From the valley there appear to be paths going straight up the fell, but these are not paths at all : they are incipient streams and runnels*) As an alternative, an old neglected track that branches from the higher path to Silver Bay is recommended: this slants leftwards to the skyline depression between Birk Fell and Grey Crag, the easy remainder of the climb then following without the help of a path. This old track is difficult to locate from above and it is better not used for descent as there is rough ground in the vicinity.

The diversion of the old track from the higher path to Silver Bay is not distinct: it occurs a full half-mile beyond the quarry at a point where there is a bluff of grey rock on the left above some larches. A flat boulder marks the junction, and a few ancient cairns along the route are a help. Botanists will find much of interest here.

Note also, 200 yards up the old track, a faint path turning away on the right: this climbs high across the face below Grey Crag, is lost on scree, but can be traced beyond, on the 1500' contour, all the way to the usual route via Boardale Hause — an exhilarating high-level walk. From this path the summit may be gained without difficulty *after leaving Grey Crag behind and crossing a small ravine.*

On the Boardale Hause route, take the upper path at the fork near the seat. Watch for the zigzag: if this is missed the walker naturally gravitates to the lower path. The prominent ashtree is on the *upper* path.

One cannot sojourn at Patterdale without looking at Place Fell and one cannot look long at Place Fell without duly setting forth to climb it. The time is very well spent.

ASCENT FROM SANDWICK
1700 feet of ascent : 2½ miles

An ascent direct from Boardale may be made most easily by the path leaving the barn above Nettleslack.

PLACE FELL

Top of Grey Crag

The Knight

grass   beacon

groove   Mortar Crag

Low Moss   sheepfold   grass

Birk Fell

sheepfold

ravine

BOARDALE HAUSE

High Dodd   ruin

← path starts directly opposite barn

Scalehow Beck

beacon

groove

Sleet Fell   groove

Scalehow Force
PATTERDALE (path 3)

barn

wall

← path starts indistinctly 100 yards beyond gate

ruin
Nettleslack   barn

Boardale Beck

gate   bracken

barn

Ullswater

east track

pastures

HOWTOWN (road) 1½   sign post   ruin   barn

Sandwick Beck   Sandwick

HOWTOWN (path) 1¾

looking south·west

Five alternatives are shown for the initial part of the climb, the best on a clear day being the pathless route over the top of Sleet Fell (which is steep). All ways converge near the sheepfold on Low Moss, beyond which is a further choice.

THE SUMMIT
A rocky ridge overtops gently-rising slopes and has a cairn at one end and a triangulation column at the other. Many tarns adorn the top of the fell.
DESCENTS: Routes of descent are indicated in the illustration of the view; that to Boardale Hause is safest in bad weather.

Place Fell 7

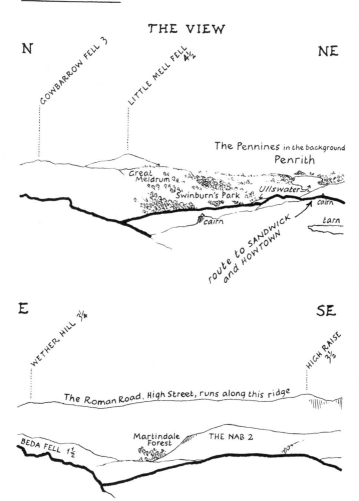

THE VIEW

N   NE

COWBARROW FELL 3

LITTLE MELL FELL 4½

The Pennines in the background

Penrith

Great Meldrum 2

Swinburn's Park

Ullswater

cairn

cairn

route to SANDWICK and HOWTOWN

tarn

E   SE

WETHER HILL 2¾

HIGH RAISE 3½

The Roman Road, High Street, runs along this ridge

Martindale Forest

THE NAB 2

BEDA FELL 1½

The thick line marks the visible boundaries
of Place Fell from the summit cairn.
The figures following the names of fells
indicate distances in miles.

THE VIEW

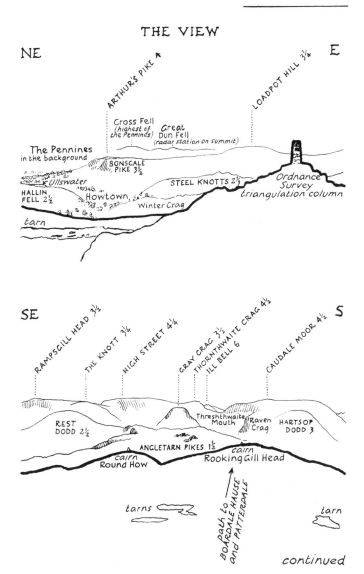

NE

ARTHUR'S PIKE

Cross Fell
(highest of
the Pennines)

Great
Dun Fell
(radar station on summit)

LOADPOT HILL 3¼

E

The Pennines
in the background

BONSCALE
PIKE 3½

Ullswater

STEEL KNOTTS 2⅓

Ordnance
Survey
triangulation column

HALLIN
FELL 2½

Howtown

Winter Crag

tarn

SE

RAMPSGILL HEAD 3½

THE KNOTT 3¼

HIGH STREET 4¼

GRAY CRAG 3½
THORNTHWAITE CRAG 4½
ILL BELL 6

CAUDALE MOOR 4½

S

REST
DODD 2½

Threshthwaite
Mouth

Raven
Crag

HARTSOP
DODD 3

ANGLETARN PIKES 1½

cairn
Round How

cairn
Rooking Gill Head

tarns

tarn

PATH to BOARDALE HAUSE
and PATTERDALE

continued

THE VIEW

continued
S   **SW**

RED SCREES 5 · LITTLE HART CRAG 4½ · DOVE CRAG 4½ · HART CRAG 4¼ · FAIRFIELD 4⅓

MIDDLE DODD 4½
Kirkstone Pass
Brothers Water
HARTSOP ABOVE HOW 3½
Deepdale
ARNISON CRAG 1½
BIRKS 2
Glemara Park

A steep, rough descent may be made to Patterdale over this edge, but there is no path. The Boardale Hause route is to be preferred, and takes no longer

W   **NW**

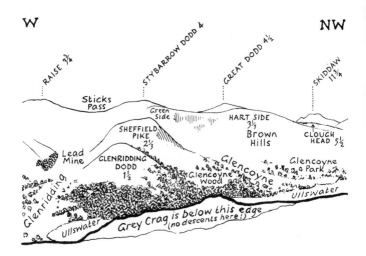

RAISE 2¾ · STYBARROW DODD 4 · GREAT DODD 4½ · SKIDDAW 11¼

Sticks Pass
Green Side
HART SIDE 3⅓
Brown Hills
CLOUGH HEAD 5½
SHEFFIELD PIKE 2⅓
Lead Mine
GLENRIDDING DODD 1½
Glencoyne
Glencoyne Wood
Glencoyne Park
Glenridding
Ullswater
Ullswater
Grey Crag is below this edge (no descents here!)

THE VIEW

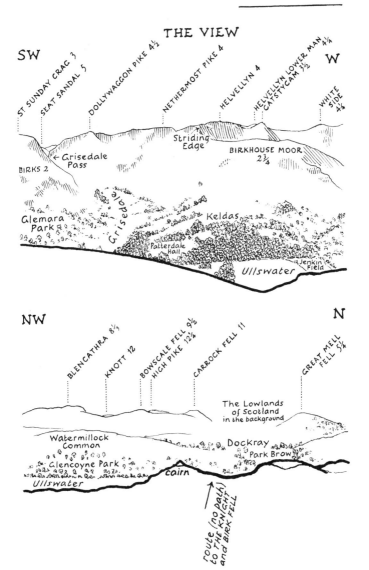

Rampsgill Head

2581'

Spelt 'Ramsgill Head' on
the Ordnance Survey maps.
Local writers include the 'p'.

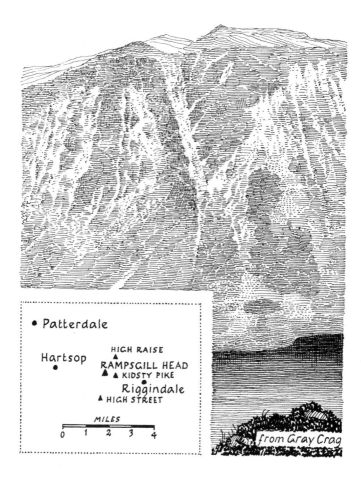

• Patterdale

HIGH RAISE
▲
Hartsop   RAMPSGILL HEAD
•   ▲ ▲ KIDSTY PIKE
          •
          Riggindale
          ▲ HIGH STREET

MILES
0   1   2   3   4

from Gray Crag

NATURAL FEATURES

There is usually little difficulty in defining the boundaries of a mountain. If it rises in isolation there is no difficulty, and even if it is merely a high point on a ridge invariably its main slopes go down to valley-level, probably on both flanks, and the limit of its extent in other directions is, as a rule, marked by watercourses falling from the cols or depressions linking it with adjacent heights. Rampsgill Head is, geographically, a 'key' point in the High Street range, for two independent ridges of some importance leave its summit, and it is, therefore, all the more remarkable that a neat and precise definition of its natural boundaries cannot be given, largely because lower secondary summits on the side ridges are also regarded as separate fells and claim to themselves territory that would otherwise be attributed to the parent fell. It is also unusual for so prominent a height to be without an official name. Rampsgill Head is properly the name of the semicircle of high ground enclosing the rough upper reaches of the valley of Rampsgill but is now generally attached to all the fell above and beyond, although occasionally some writers have remedied the lack of a common title by referring to the whole mass hereabouts, east of the watershed, as Kidsty Pike, but this is incorrect.

The most impressive natural feature is the fringe of crags breaking abruptly at the edge of the summit facing Rampsgill, and the long slopes of boulder debris and scree below are an indication that, before the age of decay, the rock-scenery here must have been very striking. Grass predominates elsewhere but there is another steep face of rock, Twopenny Crag, falling into Riggindale. Hayeswater lies at the foot of the western slope, but the principal becks from the fell act as feeders of Ullswater and Haweswater.

Twopenny Crag

This fine arête (here seen from the south) starts from a leaning pinnacle on the west face and leads directly to the top of the fell. It is littered with loose rock and is obviously in a state of decay; otherwise it would surely deserve the attention of rock-climbers

The summit crags

The eastern aspect of the arête, here illustrated, reveals a prominent vertical buttress of sound, 'clean' rock, not of great height but perhaps worth carrying a rope up from Patterdale or Hartsop

MAP

The crags above the north-west face

ASCENTS FROM PATTERDALE AND HARTSOP
2200 feet of ascent : 4½ miles from Patterdale
2050 feet of ascent : 2¼ miles from Hartsop

HIGH RAISE

RAMPSGILL HEAD

HIGH STREET

2500   grass
2400
2300

THE KNOTT

Rampsgill

REST DODD
2100

2300
2200
2100
2000
1900
1800
1700

grass

peat hags

gate

gate

HARTSOP 1½

The brief view down Bannerdale from Satura Crag is often missed. Detour left of the path to see it.

Satura Crag tarns

The valley down on the right is that of Hayeswater Gill: it descends to Hartsop.

Bannerdale

MARTINDALE

Buck Crag

gate

BROCK CRAGS

1700

For a diagram of the path from Hartsop see The Knott 3

1700

1600   Angle Tarn

PATTERDALE 2

For a diagram of the ascent to Angle Tarn from Patterdale see Angletarn Pikes 5

looking east

This is a most enjoyable excursion with a succession of widely differing views, all excellent; and the route itself, never very distinct, is an interesting puzzle to unravel. In bad weather, however, there will be some difficulty, and a stranger may run into trouble on top of Rampsgill Head, where there are crags.

ASCENT FROM MARDALE
1950 feet of ascent · 3½ miles from the road end

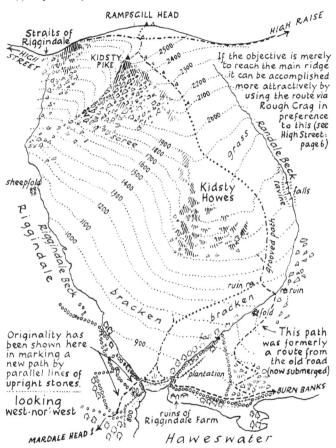

RAMPSGILL HEAD

HIGH RAISE

Straits of Riggindale

HIGH STREET

KIDSTY PIKE

2500
2400
2300
2200
2100
2000
1900
1800
1700
1600
1500
1400
1300
1200
1100
1000
900
800

If the objective is merely to reach the main ridge it can be accomplished more attractively by using the route via Rough Crag in preference to this (see High Street: page 6)

scree

grass

Randale Beck ravine

falls

Kidsty Howes

sheepfold

Riggindale

Riggindale Beck

bracken

bracken

grooved path

ruin

ruin

fold

Originality has been shown here in marking a new path by parallel lines of upright stones.

fall

This path was formerly a route from the old road (now submerged)

looking west·nor'west

plantation

BURN BANKS

MARDALE HEAD

ruins of Riggindale Farm

Haweswater

This is a dull climb over neglected and fading paths that the Haweswater project committed to lingering death. Tough grass grows on the fellsides where once both dalesfolk and visitors trod. The gaunt ruins of Riggindale are symbolic of this dying route.

THE SUMMIT

MARDALE ILL BELL   HIGH STREET   THORNTHWAITE CRAG

On the right sort of day, the top is a pleasant place to linger awhile. The turf is delightful, there is some outcropping rock to add interest, the rim of crags is worthy of a leisurely and detailed exploration, the views are good in all directions. A prominent, well-built cairn stands on the edge of the abrupt north-west face; thirty yards away is the highest cairn — an untidy heap of stones — and sixty yards further south-west is a spectral signpost that once directed visitors to Mardale and Patterdale but lost its arms long ago: in any case its usefulness would be largely past, for few now go to Mardale.

DESCENTS : For Patterdale and Hartsop, aim for The Knott to join the path there. For Mardale, use the ridge beyond Kidsty Pike — but the warning cannot be given too often until all old maps are out of circulation that Mardale Head is uninhabited, and the only beds in the valley are at the Haweswater Hotel on the far side of the lake.

In mist, the edge of the escarpment is sufficiently defined to give direction: keep it on the right hand if bound for either Patterdale or Hartsop and descend easy ground to the path. For Mardale, if the path over Kidsty Pike cannot be located, incline left and follow Randale Beck down to the valley.

RIDGE ROUTES

To HIGH RAISE, 2634': ¾ mile : NE
Depression at 2450': 190 feet of ascent
Follow the edge of the crags north-east
(noting the arête on the way) and join a
narrow path (the old High Street) that
crosses the depression and continues
up the easy grass slope of High Raise
opposite. When the stony top is
reached leave the path and
pick a way among embedded
boulders to the cairn.

To THE KNOTT, 2423': ⅓ mile : W
Depression at 2360'
65 feet of ascent
Descend the easy west slope to
the wall-corner in the depression
(the good path *crossed* here is the
regular Patterdale to High Street
route). He is tired indeed who
cannot gain the summit of The Knott from the corner of the wall, and
two minutes for the ascent is a generous time allowance.

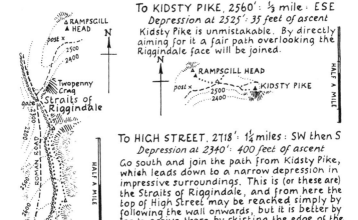

To KIDSTY PIKE, 2560': ⅓ mile : ESE
Depression at 2525': 35 feet of ascent
Kidsty Pike is unmistakable. By directly
aiming for it a fair path overlooking the
Riggindale face will be joined.

To HIGH STREET, 2718': 1¼ miles : SW then S
Depression at 2340': 400 feet of ascent
Go south and join the path from Kidsty Pike,
which leads down to a narrow depression in
impressive surroundings. This is (or these are)
the Straits of Riggindale, and from here the
top of High Street may be reached simply by
following the wall onwards, but it is better by
far to arrive there by skirting the edge of the
cliffs on the left, which gives striking views.

All these routes are easy, and, with care, safe in mist

THE VIEW

Although the Helvellyn range conceals most of the western fells the view is very extensive and interesting. There is a commanding prospect of Rampsgill from the larger cairn.

Principal Fells

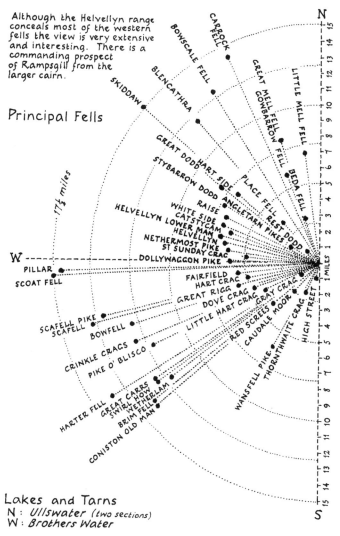

Lakes and Tarns
N : *Ullswater (two sections)*
W : *Brothers Water*

THE VIEW

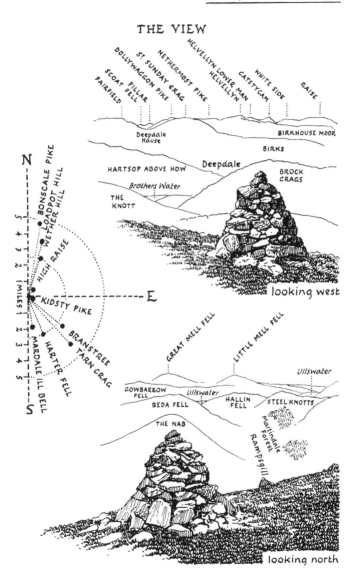

FAIRFIELD
SCOAT PILLAR FELL
DOLLYWAGGON PIKE
ST SUNDAY CRAG
NETHERMOST PIKE
HELVELLYN LOWER MAN
HELVELLYN
CATSTYCAM
WHITE SIDE
RAISE

Deepdale Hause

BIRKHOUSE MOOR

BIRKS

Deepdale

HARTSOP ABOVE HOW

BROCK CRAGS

Brothers Water

THE KNOTT

looking west

N

S 5 4 3 2 1MILES 1 2 3 4 5

BONSCALE PIKE
LOADPOT HILL
WETHER HILL

HIGH RAISE

E

KIDSTY PIKE

BRANSTREE
TARN CRAG

HARTER FELL

MARDALE ILL BELL

GREAT MELL FELL

LITTLE MELL FELL

Ullswater

GOWBARROW FELL

Ullswater

BEDA FELL

HALLIN FELL

STEEL KNOTTS

THE NAB

Martindale Forest

Rampsgill

looking north

Rest Dodd

2278'

from Gray Crag

Howtown •
•
Martindale
▲ BEDA FELL

• Patterdale
ANGLETARN PIKES
▲   REST DODD
▲
Hartsop   ▲ HIGH
•   RAISE
▲ THE KNOTT

MILES
0   1   2   3   4

NATURAL FEATURES

The steep-sided ridge that divides Martindale into the secluded upper valleys of Bannerdale and Rampsgill rises first to the shapely conical summit of The Nab and then more gradually to the rounded dome of Rest Dodd, which dominates both branches. It is a fell of little interest, although the east flank falls spectacularly in fans of colourful scree. Rest Dodd stands at an angle on the undulating grassy ridge coming down from the main watershed to the shores of Ullswater, and its south-west slope, which drains into Hayeswater Gill, is crossed by the track from Patterdale to High Street. Much of the fell is within the Martindale deer forest.

MAP

ASCENT FROM HARTSOP
1700 feet of ascent : 2 miles

REST DODD

looking east

Note here the unusual junction of walls

grass

peat-hags

grass

Satura Crag

PATTERDALE

HIGH STREET

gap

ford

cascades

Prison Crag

gate

stile

filter house

pipeline

gate

Wath Bridge

gate ruin

HAYESWATER

Sulphury Gill

Hayeswater Gill

Walker Bridge

Low Hartsop

The usual path up the valley (to Hayeswater) runs along the right (south) side of the gill above Wath Bridge, but if the beck is in spate the ford may be impassable and it is then advisable to keep on the left side, passing the filter house. Alternative routes are shown for the final climb up the fellside but no amount of inventiveness can make this dull trudge interesting or attractive. Another approach is by way of Satura Crag, using the path traversing the flank of Brock Crags (see Brock Crags 2)

Initially the approach is good, for the valley of Hayeswater Gill is both beautiful and interesting, but beyond the quality of the scene deteriorates sadly.

ASCENT FROM PATTERDALE
1900 feet of ascent : 3½ miles

Take the usual route to High Street (*diagrams, Angletarn Pikes 5 and High Street 5*), which traverses the slopes of Rest Dodd, but after crossing the top of Satura Crag, continue by the wall directly ahead, bearing left at the top.

(It is an interesting fact that the Patterdale–High Street route formerly followed this wall up to its top corner and down the south slope of Rest Dodd, an extra 300 feet of climbing which the present more direct path avoids. No traces remain of a path by the wall.)

THE SUMMIT

A summit-cairn with a flagpole! Such is Rest Dodd's distinction, but not even this brave decoration relieves the drabness of the top of the fell. There are three cairns and a natural obstacle in the shape of an eroded peat-hag on the grassy summit.

DESCENTS : Go down past the south cairn to the wall corner (or, more properly, the junction of two walls). Follow the wall west, and at its end will be found the path from High Street to Patterdale. Do not attempt any descents into Rampsgill, which is deer forest.

Buck Crag and Heck Crag from Satura Crag

THE VIEW

The view is neither so pleasing nor so extensive as that from The Knott nearby, although the full length of the Helvellyn range is well seen. The wild and lonely head of Rampsgill is an impressive sight. In the west, Great Gable fits snugly into the deep depression of Deepdale Hause.

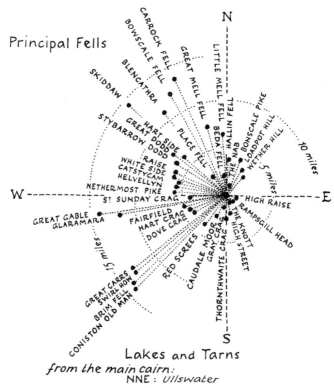

Principal Fells

Lakes and Tarns

from the main cairn:
 NNE : *Ullswater*

from the south cairn:
 S : *Hayeswater*
 WSW : *Brothers Water*

from the west cairn:
 NNE : *Ullswater*
 WSW : *Brothers Water*
 WNW : *Angle Tarn*

RIDGE ROUTES

To ANGLETARN PIKES, 1857': 1¾ miles: W, then NW
Depression at 1600': 300 feet of ascent

An interesting walk, full of variety. From the west cairn go down the shoulder to Satura Crag, where the path to Patterdale is joined. (In mist, descend by the wall). Leave the path by the beck flowing into Angle Tarn. A boggy plateau is skirted on the right. Of the many tops the furthest is the main Pike.

To THE KNOTT, 2423': ¾ mile: SSE
Depression at 1925': 500 feet of ascent
Merely a matter of following a wall.
From the south cairn the wall is soon reached (150 yards south). The depression is marshy. The High Street path is crossed at a gate.

The Nab is completely within the Martindale Deer Forest.
IT IS OUT OF BOUNDS FOR WALKERS

To THE NAB, 1887': 1¼ miles
NW, then E and N
*Depression at 1650'
250 feet of ascent*
The way of the trespasser is hard, for this route is really unpleasant: the depression is a vast morass.

These notes and diagram are given only for the sake of completeness of records; no inducement to trespass is intended.

Sallows

better known locally as Kentmere Park

from Badger Rock

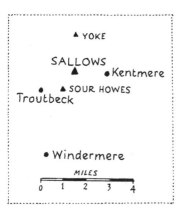

▲ YOKE

SALLOWS ▲ • Kentmere

• Troutbeck ▲ SOUR HOWES

• Windermere

MILES

0   1   2   3   4

For most walkers, the fells proper in this region start at Garburn Pass and rise to the north, but there are two hills, twins almost, immediately to the south of the Pass, worth a mention although these are not strictly walkers' territory. The higher of the two is named Sallows (on all maps), bounding the Pass, and has much merit as a viewpoint and a scantier virtue as a grouse sanctuary. It is not worth the detour for anyone bound for Ill Bell and places north, and, in any case, there is not entirely free access to the fell and visitors may be requested to state their business

MAP

Garburn Pass
gate
gate
Kentmere
gate
ruin
Hall Gill
gate
Badger Rock
gate
gate
Church
gap
gap
1400
1300
1200
1500
1600
gate
Kentmere Hall
gate
Cowsty Beck
× SALLOWS 1691'
old quarry
Kentmere Park
Scandale
Hall Gill
1400
Long Crag
1300
1200
Scour Rigg
800
Whiteside End
resvr
1000
River Kent
road to KENTMERE 1¼
Capple Howe
butts
×× × × ×
1300
1200
1100
1000
plank bridge
900
shooting hut
gate
Kentmere Hall Plantation (private)
Diatomite Works
Waterford Bridge
The southern boundary of Sallows is Park Beck. The map is extended to enable more detail of the routes from Staveley and Ings to be given.
gate
gates
gate
Park Beck
Black Beck
800
ruin
×
Private paths in Kentmere Park and Woods are omitted.
N
Mickle Moss
gate
Croft Head
Ullthwaite Bridge
gate
gate
800
Browfoot
STAVELEY 2 (road)
STAVELEY 2
ONE MILE
INGS 1½
INGS 1½
700
600
STAVELEY 2

A : INGS via GRASSGARTH
B : INGS via HUGILL HALL

ASCENTS

The summit may be most easily and quickly visited from the top of Garburn Pass, where a gateway in the wall (without a gate, but barricaded) gives access to the fell. Alternatively it can be gained by a mile-long ascent from the Ings-Kentmere Hall bridle-path: a simple gradient, but not easy walking.

Sallows is not, as it appears to be, a 'short cut' to Garburn Pass from the south. Apart from doubts as to trespass, its tough heather slopes compel slow progress, and time will be lost. Garburn is best reached by orthodox routes.

THE SUMMIT

A curious curving mound of shale and grass, thirty feet long and narrow as a parapet, marks the highest part of the fell: it seems to be man-made, but is more probably a natural formation. It has no cairn. Heather and coarse grass cover the top of the fell, but there are small outcrops of rock west of the summit.

The summit mound

THE VIEW

The Lakeland scene occupies only half the panorama: it is outstandingly good to the west but unattractive northwards where Yoke fills much of the horizon. The rest of the view is exceedingly extensive, varied and interesting, covering a wide area from the Pennines across Morecambe Bay to Black Combe.

Principal Fells

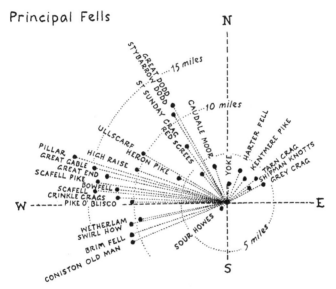

Lakes and Tarns: SSW: Windermere

Sallows from Ullthwaite Bridge

Selside Pike

2142'

Haweswater Hotel
●

● Swindale Head

Mardale   ▲ SELSIDE PIKE
Head ●

▲ BRANSTREE

▲ HARTER FELL

MILES

0   1   2   3   4

from Mosedale Beck
near the waterfalls

NATURAL FEATURES

One of the lesser-known fells is Selside Pike on the eastern fringe of the district, commanding the head of the shy and beautiful little valley of Swindale. Its neglect is scarcely merited, for although the summit is a dull grass mound with little reward in views the fell has an extremely rugged eastern face that closes the valley in dramatic fashion: here are dark crags, rarely-visited waterfalls, a curious dry tarn-bed set amongst moraines and, above it, a perfect hanging valley, the two being connected by a very formidable gully.

For countless ages Selside Pike has looked down upon Swindale and seen there a picture of unspoiled charm. Now the engineers have taken over the valley — they may not spoil it, but it is more certain that they can not improve it. Swindale is almost the only remaining Lakeland valley that does not cater for the motorist. Please, Manchester, leave it as nearly as you found it!

Selside Pike from the old corpse-road

Selside Pike 3

MAP

Once upon a time, the Corpse Road was the route by which Mardale's dead were taken, by horseback, for burial at Shap; the last such journey was made in 1736.

N

ONE MILE

HAWESWATER HOTEL 1¼
BAMPTON 5 (road)

MARDALE
COMMON

old corpse-road

continuation opposite

Haweswater

gate

ruin
cairns
ruin

falls

Hogill Beck

MARDALE HEAD
(road)

BRANSTREE

fold

SELSIDE
PIKE 2142'

continuation
BRANSTREE 3

Swindale
with Selside Pike at the head of the valley

MAP

SWINDALE COMMON

old corpse road

post

fold

Selside End

ruins

Dodd Bottom

SWINDALE HEAD
ROSGILL 3½ (road)

gate

Swindale Head

Swindale Beck

Swindale

Simon Stone

falls

falls

N

ONE MILE

cairns

gate

900

1000

1100

1200

1300

1400

1500

700

800

900

1000

slate cairn

SELSIDE PIKE
2142'

Nabs Moor

2100

2000

Hobgrumble Gill

gate

sheepfolds

Mosedale Beck

continuation opposite

continuation BRANSTREE 4

slate cairn
overlooking
Swindale

Swindale Head

ASCENT FROM SWINDALE HEAD
1200 feet of ascent : 1½ miles (via the north-east ridge)
1350 feet of ascent : 2¼ miles (via the Mosedale path)

looking south-south-west

The quality of the scenery deteriorates when the tedious higher slopes are reached. If returning to Swindale, ascend by the ridge and descend by the wire fence, making a detour to see the waterfalls.

THE SUMMIT

It is surprising to find a cairn of several tons of stones where all else is grass, and it seems likely that originally there was a rock outcrop here that has been broken up and formed into a cairn. 10 yards away is an angle in the fence, which is a guide, in mist, to Mosedale or Branstree

THE VIEW

The view towards Lakeland is disappointing, being confined to the surroundings of Mardale except for a glimpse of distant fells over the Straits of Riggindale.
Eastwards, however, there is a splendid prospect of the Pennines, with Shap village prominent.

Principal Fells

LOADPOT HILL
WETHER HILL
HIGH RAISE
RAMPSGILL HEAD
KIDSTY PIKE
NETHERMOST PIKE
ST SUNDAY CRAG
10 miles
1½ miles
5 miles
2½ miles
HIGH STREET
THORNTHWAITE CRAG
MARDALE ILL BELL
HARTER FELL
BRANSTREE
N
S
W
E

Lakes and Tarns

NNW : *Haweswater*
Small Water and *Blea Water* can both be seen by walking 30 yards W in the direction of High Street.
And if *Swindale Reservoir* materialises, there will be an excellent full-length view of it from the slate cairn NE.

RIDGE ROUTE

To BRANSTREE, 2333′ : 1½ miles : SW
Two shallow depressions : 450 feet of ascent
    An easy walk on grass ; safe in mist
The only objects of interest on this dull trudge are man-made : the old survey post and the fine cairn on Artlecrag Pike. The 2209′ summit is hardly worth traversing although it has (which the main summits have not) a view of Helvellyn. *In mist keep to the fence.*

SELSIDE PIKE
2100
2100
N
grass
2000
2100
peat-bed (or tarn)
2209′
2200
2200
Artlecrag Pike
survey post
2100
BRANSTREE
2300
2300
2100
HALF A MILE

Shipman Knotts

1926'

from Stockdale

Shipman Knotts is of moderate altitude and would have called for no more than the brief comment that it is a shoulder of Kentmere Pike had it not earned for itself a separate chapter by reason of the characteristic roughnesses of its surface. Rocky outcrops are everywhere on the steep slopes, persisting even in the woods of Sadgill, although these seldom attain the magnitude of crags. This fell is usually climbed on the way to Harter Fell from the south, and its rock should be welcomed for there is precious little beyond. The south slope carries the path from Kentmere to Longsleddale

▲ HARTER FELL

KENTMERE ▲ TARN
▲ ILL BELL ▲ PIKE ▲ CRAG

▲ GREY
SHIPMAN KNOTTS CRAG

● Kentmere

Longsleddale ●

0   1   2   3   4

MAP

The cart-track linking Stile End and Sadgill
is the regular highway between Kentmere
and Longsleddale; a line of telegraph posts
accompanies it. Highest point: 1120 feet.

ONE MILE

ASCENTS

from Kentmere : 1400 feet of ascent : 2¼ miles
from Sadgill : 1300 feet of ascent : 1½ miles

Shipman Knotts is usually climbed as a means of
gaining access to the Harter Fell ridge, but is an
interesting short expedition in itself. The ascent
is most easily made alongside the wall running up
from the summit of the Stile End-Sadgill 'pass'; but
from Kentmere the ridge north of the fell-top may
be reached by a grooved path leaving Hollowbank.
Safe in mist if the wall route is followed.

The summit from the south

THE SUMMIT

KENTMERE PIKE

Three rocky knolls, on the east side of the wall, form the summit, and of these the middle one is highest. It is without a cairn.

DESCENTS: Cross the wall and follow it south to the pass, where turn left for Longsleddale, right for Kentmere. In mist, this is a safe route

The summit-ridge from Goat Scar

THE VIEW

The northern half of the panorama is restricted to nearby heights of greater elevation; the southern is open, extensive and pleasing. There is a good view of Longsleddale.

Principal Fells

Lakes and Tarns

S : Skeggles Water
SW : Windermere
The small sheet of water SSW is part of the diatomite workings in Kentmere

RIDGE ROUTE

To KENTMERE PIKE, 2397':
1¼ miles : N then NW
Depression at 1875'
525 feet of ascent
Easy walking, safe in mist
Follow the wall and fence, with a detour to the cairn on Goat Scar for the view. The scenery of the depression is impressive

------

A word about SADGILL (for artists)—
A typical Lakeland scene of great charm is that of the picturesque hamlet of Sadgill in its bower of trees below the towering mass of Goat Scar with the arched bridge in front.

Sour Howes

1568'

better known locally as
Applethwaite Common

from Troutbeck

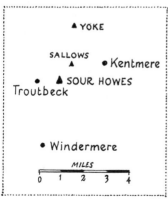

▲ YOKE

SALLOWS
● Kentmere

●
Troutbeck   ▲ SOUR HOWES

● Windermere

MILES
0   1   2   3   4

Although all maps agree that
the summit of this fell is named
Sour Howes, its broadest flank,
carrying the Garburn Pass Road
down to Troutbeck, is far better
known as Applethwaite Common;
this flank is traversed also by
the pleasant Dubbs Road. There
is little about the fell to attract
walkers, and nothing to justify
a detour from the main Ill Bell
ridge to the north, for although
the views are really good they
are better from the main ridge.
There is heather on the eastern
slopes, and therefore, inevitably,
grouse; and therefore, inevitably,
shooting butts: one may admire
the construction of these butts
while deploring their purpose.

MAP

If approaching from Troutbeck, note that the Garburn Road starts as a narrow stony lane leaving the main road 250 yards south of the church.

ASCENTS

Sour Howes is a fell with no obvious appeal to walkers, and few other than conscientious guide-book writers will visit its summit; nevertheless it makes a pleasant walk from Windermere, Ings or Staveley, especially on a clear day for the views are good.

Two lanes leave Ings (one via Grassgarth and one via Hugill Hall) and another leaves Browfoot (two miles up the Kentmere valley from Staveley): these join, and at the terminus the old bridle-path to Kentmere Hall may be followed for a mile, when it may be forsaken and a way made to the top by the shooting-butts, using the stiles to cross the walls.

An enchanting path leaves High Borrans, climbing first through juniper bushes, then bracken, then heather; when it peters out keep to the route shown on the map.

The summit is easily visited from the top of Garburn Pass: here a gap in the wall (a gateway without a gate) gives access to the enclosure containing the highest point.

THE SUMMIT

The top of the fell is a series of grass hummocks. The highest of these is in the form of a ridge with walls of exposed shaly rock, especially to the east, and is crowned by a few stones, hardly enough to deserve the name of cairn.

Red Screes from Sour Howes

THE VIEW

The crowded skyline in the west arrests the attention, with the vertical profile of Scafell above Mickledore prominent in the scene. Langdale Pikes are well seen between and below Great End and Great Gable. There is a very extensive and beautiful prospect southwards from the far Pennines round to Morecambe Bay and Black Combe.

Principal Fells

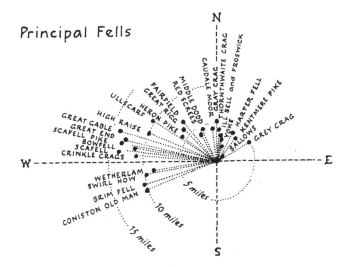

Lakes and Tarns
S: *Borrans Reservoir*
SSW: *Windermere*

Most old and disused quarries are gloomy and repellant places but Applethwaite Quarry, near the Garburn Road, is relieved from desolation by a planting of conifers and a magnificent view. An interesting feature is the old weighbridge, now overgrown. A favourite with foxes, this quarry!

Applethwaite Quarry

Steel Knotts

1414'

summit named Pikeawassa

from Howe Grain Beck

Wether Hill's western flank swells into a bulge, Gowk Hill, which itself sends out a crooked bony arm northwards to form a lofty independent ridge running parallel to the main range and enclosing with it the short hidden valley of Fusedale. On the crest of this ridge, rock is never far from the surface and it breaks through in several places, notably at the highest point, which is a craggy tor that would worthily embellish the summit of many a higher fell. This freakish gnarled ridge is Steel Knotts; the summit-tor is named, on the best of authority, (but not by many, one imagines) Pikeawassa. (O.S. 1" and 2½" maps)

Howtown
●
STEEL KNOTTS
▲   ▲ LOADPOT
          HILL
         ▲ WETHER HILL

MILES

0   1   2   3

MAP

ASCENTS

FROM HOWTOWN: The natural route of ascent is by the craggy ridge above Howtown. This has an intimidating aspect but it is without perils and gives an exhilarating scramble. Leave the path at its base by a concrete waterworks notice inscribed thus: 8 AV 5 and climb upwards between the rocks; initially there is a track obscured by bracken. A cairn surmounts the steepest part of the ridge and the walking is then easy to the top of the fell.

FROM LANTY TARN: A pronounced shoulder, with two tiers of crag, descends north-west to Lanty Tarn and offers a less satisfactory route. From the tarn (a shallow pond) climb to the right (south) of the crags to a cairn above them. An easy slope then follows.

FROM MARTINDALE OLD CHURCH: This is the easiest way. Climb the fellside by the church to a good path slanting upwards (this is the Martindale path to the High Street range). Leave the path at a wall and turn up left to the ridge and again left to the top.

Although Steel Knotts is of small extent and modest elevation, it should not be climbed in mist. If caught by mist on the top, descend south to the wall and return by the path to Martindale Old Church.

THE SUMMIT

Steel Knotts may well claim to have the sharpest summit in Lakeland, for the rock tor (Pikeawassa) that crowns the top is so acute that only very agile walkers will be able to stand upon it, although, it will be noted, it is a popular perch for birds. There is no cairn.

STEEL KNOTTS
(PIKEAWASSA)

MARTINDALE

HOWTOWN

Fusedale Beck

ravine

× ruin

1500

Gowk Hill

N

ONE MILE

1100
1200
1300
1100
1200
1300
1300
1400
1500

groove

levels

groove

HIGH STREET (ROMAN ROAD)

▲ WETHER HILL

2200

1600 1700 1800 1900 2000 2100

Keasgill Head
peat hags

RIDGE ROUTE

To WETHER HILL, 2210'

1½ miles : S, then SSE, SE and NNE
Depression at 1200' : 1100 feet of ascent

An easy walk, followed by a dull climb
Follow the ridge south, joining a fair track to a ruined hut at the foot of the final slope, which may be tackled anywhere although it is preferable to use one of the grooves. This walk is safe in mist.

Incidentally, this is the best way onto the High Street range from Martindale or Howtown, whether or not the summits of Steel Knotts and Wether Hill are visited. (The Keasgill groove is the usual one)

THE VIEW

Principal Fells

This is the best viewpoint for the upper Martindale district, the highlight of a charming scene being the confluence of the remote Rampsgill and Bannerdale valleys

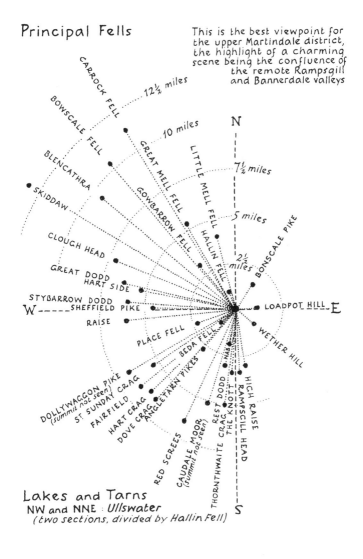

CARROCK FELL
BOWSCALE FELL
BLENCATHRA
SKIDDAW
CLOUGH HEAD
GREAT DODD
HART SIDE
STYBARROW DODD
SHEFFIELD PIKE
RAISE
W
GREAT MELL FELL
GOWBARROW FELL
LITTLE MELL FELL
HALLIN FELL
N
12½ miles
10 miles
7½ miles
5 miles
2½ miles
BONSCALE PIKE
LOADPOT HILL E
PLACE FELL
BEDA FELL
NAB
WETHER HILL
DOLLYWAGGON PIKE (summit not seen)
ST. SUNDAY CRAG
FAIRFIELD
HART CRAG
DOVE CRAG
ANGLETARN PIKES
RED SCREES
CAUDALE MOOR (summit not seen)
THORNTHWAITE CRAG
REST DODD
THE NOTT
RAMPSGILL HEAD
HIGH RAISE
S

Lakes and Tarns
NW and NNE : *Ullswater*
(two sections, divided by Hallin Fell)

Tarn Crag

2176'

Shap •

• Swindale Head

Mardale
Head •
    ▲ BRANSTREE
    ▲ HARTER FELL
       • Wet
       Sleddale

▲ **TARN CRAG**
▲ KENTMERE
  PIKE
    ▲ GREY CRAG

      • road
      summit

Longsleddale

MILES

0 1 2 3 4 5

from Sadgill Wood

NATURAL FEATURES

The gradually rising wall of fells bounding Longsleddale on the east reaches its greatest elevation, and its terminus, in Tarn Crag. To the valley this fell presents a bold front, with Buckbarrow Crag a conspicuous object, but on other sides it is uninteresting, especially eastwards where easy slopes merge into the desolate plateaux of Shap Fells. It is enclosed on the north by the wide, shallow depression of Mosedale, a natural pass linking Longsleddale with Swindale in wild and lonely surroundings: here a solitary shepherd's cottage merely accentuates the utter dreariness of the scene. (Yet on rare occasions of soft evening light even Mosedale can look inexpressibly beautiful!). The walker hereabouts will be in no doubt, without reference to his map, that he has passed outside the verge of Lakeland.

looking north-east

1 : The summit
2 : Ridge continuing to Grey Crag
3 : Ridge continuing to Branstree
4 : Buckbarrow Crag   5 : Galeforth Brow
6 : Brunt Tongue   7 : Greycrag Tarn
8 : Galeforth Gill   9 : River Sprint
10 : Little Mosedale Beck   13 : Mosedale
11 : Mosedale Beck   12 : Longsleddale

The head of Longsleddale

Tarn Crag 3

MAP

MAP

SWINDALE 2

plank bridge

SHAP 6 (distinct path)

1400

ONE MILE

Mosedale Beck

falls

Brunt Tongue

1500

N

1700

1600

Little Mosedale Beck

1800

continuation opposite

ASCENT FROM LONGSLEDDALE
1600 feet of ascent
2 miles from Sadgill

An interesting walk, *but dangerous in mist.* The ascent from the top of the quarry-road is much the easier. There are no paths on the fell.

For fuller details of the Great Howe route, see GREY CRAG 4

TARN CRAG

GREY CRAG

GATESCARTH PASS

MOSEDALE

2000

1900

Greycrag Tarn

1800

gate

ruin

Buckbarrow Crag

1700

an excellent viewpoint for Longsleddale

Great Howe

1600

rock gorge pools and waterfalls

stile

fold

plantations

1500

1400

1300

1200

1100

Galeforth Gill

1000

900

800

gully

quarry road

River Sprint

boulders

gates

gate

ruin

looking north-east

Longsleddale

CARNETT BRIDGE 5

Sadgill

OTHER ASCENTS:
From Swindale or Shap, the obvious route
  of approach is by Brunt Tongue, an easy ascent.
From the Kendal-Shap Road, the various routes
  pass first over Grey Crag (*for details see* GREY CRAG 5 *and* 6)
  Clear, settled weather is essential on these unfrequented approaches

THE SUMMIT

Not until Manchester Corporation's engineers climbed Tarn Crag, in the course of their duty, and departed from it for the last time, did its summit acquire distinction: the wide dreary top then found itself left with a curious structure — a high wooden platform with a core of stone and concrete, which served for a time as a survey post during the construction of the Longsleddale tunnel conveying the Haweswater Aqueduct south. Now, thirty years later, the aqueduct is in place and the scars are gone from the valley — but the hoary survey post still stands, defying the weather and puzzling the few travellers who come this way and find no clue as to its purpose.

The highest part of the fell, marked by a small undistinguished cairn, is a hundred yards away, to the east.

DESCENTS : The routes of ascent should be used for descent. *In mist*, keep strictly to the fences. Crags obstruct the direct way down into Longsleddale. Eastwards, Shap Fells are a wilderness to avoid in bad weather.

THE VIEW

Anyone who climbs Tarn Crag for a view of Lakeland will be very disappointed, for, excepting the Coniston fells, nothing is to be seen of the distant west because of the adjacent heights across the deep trench of Longsleddale. On a clear day there is ample recompense, however, in the excellent panorama from east round to south — where, for a hundred miles, the noble skyline of the Pennines and the wide seascape of Morecambe Bay present themselves to view without obstruction.

Principal Fells

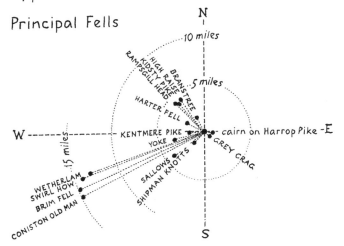

Lakes and Tarns: SW: *Windermere*

Kentmere Pike across Longsleddale

RIDGE ROUTES

To BRANSTREE, 2333' : 1¾ miles : N, then NW
Depression at 1650' : 700 feet of ascent
Rough grass, but easy gradients ; safe in mist

This is a long, featureless walk: interest is confined to the views of Longsleddale and Harter Fell. Traces of a cart-track may indicate the route taken up the easy slope of Tarn Crag for the transport of material when the survey post was under construction. Keep to the left of the wall on Branstree for the best views, to the right of it for shelter from rain.

To GREY CRAG, 2093'
¾ mile : NE, then SE and S
Depression at 1940' :
170 feet of ascent

An easy walk, best accomplished by following the fence across the depression to avoid the marsh that masquerades as Greycrag Tarn. In mist, Grey Crag is better left alone.

BRANSTREE

2300
2200
2100
2000
1900
1800
grass

1700
SWINDALE and SHAP

gate
1700
peat hags

LONGSLEDDALE

ONE MILE

N

Traces of cart-track
1800
1900
2000
2100

grass

2000
TARN CRAG
× survey post

2000
peat hags
Greycrag Tarn
GREY CRAG

from Goat Scar   TARN CRAG   from Shipman Knotts

Buckbarrow Crag

Thornthwaite Crag 2569'

CAUDALE MOOR

HIGH STREET

THORNTHWAITE CRAG

ILL BELL

Hartsop

Kentmere

Troutbeck

MILES
0 1 2 3 4

from Caudale Moor

NATURAL FEATURES

Occupying a commanding position overlooking four valleys, Thornthwaite Crag is one of the better-known fells east of Kirkstone, owing not a little of its fame to its tall pillar of stones, a landmark for miles around. Its name derives from the long shattered cliff facing west above the upper Troutbeck valley; there are also crags fringing the head of Hayeswater Gill and above the early meanderings of the River Kent. Apart from these roughnesses the fell is grassy, the ground to the east of the summit forming a wide plateau before rising gently to the parent height of High Street, of which Thornthwaite Crag is a subsidiary; it has, however, a ridge in its own right, this being a narrow steep-sided shoulder that ends in Gray Crag, northwards. Streams flow in three directions: north to Ullswater, south to Windermere and south-east along the Kentmere valley.

looking north.

1 : The summit
2 : Ridge continuing to High Street
3 : Ridge continuing to Caudale Moor
4 : Ridge continuing to Froswick
5 : Threshthwaite Mouth
6 : Thornthwaite Crag
7 : Gavel Crag
8 : Bleathwaite Crag
9 : Gray Crag
10 : Trout Beck

11 : River Kent
12 : Hayeswater Gill
13 : Hayeswater
14 : Pasture Beck
15 : North ridge
16 : Threshthwaite Cove

looking south·south·west

MAP

ASCENT FROM HARTSOP
2000 feet of ascent : 3¼ miles

THORNTHWAITE CRAG

CAUDALE MOOR

HIGH STREET

Threshthwaite Mouth

HIGH STREET

grass

ravine

2500
2400
2300
2200
2100
2000
1900
1800
1700
1600
1500

GRAY CRAG

Threshthwaite Cove

grass

Raven Crag

Hayeswater Gill

grass

Pasture Beck

HARTSOP DODD

Hayeswater

moraines

dam

1800
1700
1600
1500
1400
1300
1200

grass

sheepfold

Threshthwaite Glen

1100

There is shelter among the boulders below Raven Crag

Pronounce 'Threshthwaite' Thresh'et

Hayeswater is a reservoir for Penrith

In mist, use the Threshthwaite route only

looking south·south·east

stile
filter house
cart track
gate

old mine
Wath Bridge
old shaft
gate
ruin
gate

700
gate
600
gate

Low Hartsop

This is a very interesting and enjoyable expedition. Of the three routes illustrated, that *via* Hayeswater starts well but has a tame and tiring conclusion. If the return is to be made to Hartsop, Threshthwaite is the best approach, the descent being made along the north ridge over Gray Crag, which itself has an airy situation and good views.

ASCENT FROM TROUTBECK
2200 feet of ascent
5 miles via Scot Rake; 5½ via Threshthwaite Mouth

To locate Scot Rake from the angle in the wall, go straight up the slope and turn left above a small landslide, along a shelf to a distinct groove which may be followed (with some doubts) until the convex slope opens out and the path is visible climbing the fell ahead

Trout Beck, west of the Tongue, is pleasantly wooded and is recommended for the return journey. (Reach Threshthwaite Mouth from the summit by keeping to the wall)

The Romans may have experienced exciting incidents when they pioneered their route to High Street via Scot Rake but twentieth-century walkers will find it a long, dull ascent, with little to engage attention apart from the tracing of the Rake, which belongs more to history books than to the maps of today.

looking north

Scot Rake is the usual route, and the quickest, although the Rake itself is discerned better from a distance than when underfoot. The ascent is on grass throughout.

ASCENT FROM KENTMERE RESERVOIR
1650 feet of ascent : 2 miles

THORNTHWAITE CRAG

HIGH STREET

MARDALE ILL BELL

source of River Kent

Bleathwaite Crag

2400 2300 2200 2100 2000 1900 1800

grass

scree

FROSWICK

scree gully

2100 2000 1900 1800 1700 1600 1500 1400

Gavel Crag

scree

rock shelter

Hall Cove

waterfalls

FROSWICK

ILL BELL

1300

1200

1100

sheepfold

River Kent

1000

Lingmell End

Kentmere Reservoir

dam

KENTMERE 3

When the ground steepens below Gavel Crag, three routes are feasible : that up the slope to the left, leading into a scree gully, is tedious and better used for descent; that up the nose of Gavel Crag is a rough scramble, needing hands as well as feet, with impressive views of Ill Bell and Froswick; that by the hidden Hall Cove follows the valley to its ultimate conclusion and is easiest.

The summit of Thornthwaite Crag lies to the west of the line of the main ridge and is out of sight during the ascent until the ridge is gained.

The hidden recesses at the head of the Kentmere Valley should be a place of pilgrimage, at least once in a lifetime, for Kendal folk, for here they may witness the birth and infancy of their river. But alas, Morecambe is a greater attraction — and Hall Cove remains lonely.

looking north·north·west

This approach leads into the unfrequented dalehead of Kentmere and abounds in interest and variety all the way from the village. Rainsborrow Crag, up on the left, is a tremendous object *en route*, and Ill Bell and Froswick reveal themselves most effectively.

THE SUMMIT

Thornthwaite Beacon

It is sometimes difficult to recall the details of familiar summits but surely all who have climbed Thornthwaite Crag will identify it in memory by its remarkable 14-feet column, one of the most distinctive cairns in Lakeland. It stands in the angle of a wall that traverses the summit. A few outcrops of flaky rock in the vicinity relieve the general grassiness of the top of the fell.

DESCENTS: In clear weather all the routes of ascent may be reversed, but that to Kentmere *via* Gavel Crag is not suggested nor should routes be 'invented' as there is rough ground about. *In bad conditions*, descend to Troutbeck or Hartsop *via* Threshthwaite Mouth — to which the wall leads when followed north-west. For Kentmere, go to the end of the wall eastwards; here turn right along a faint path for 200 yards to a scree gully on the left, which descend.

looking north to Ullswater

Threshthwaite Mouth

looking south to Windermere

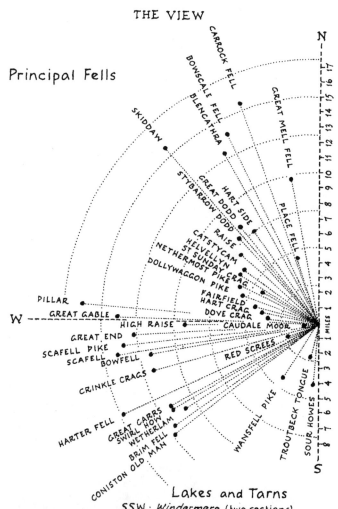

THE VIEW

Principal Fells

N

CARROCK FELL
BOWSCALE FELL
BLENCATHRA
SKIDDAW
GREAT MELL FELL
HART SIDE
GREAT DODD
STYBARROW DODD
RAISE
PLACE FELL
CATSTYCAM
HELVELLYN
ST SUNDAY CRAG
NETHERMOST PIKE
DOLLYWAGGON PIKE
FAIRFIELD
HART CRAG
PILLAR
GREAT GABLE
DOVE CRAG
HIGH RAISE
CAUDALE MOOR
W
GREAT END
SCAFELL PIKE
SCAFELL
BOWFELL
RED SCREES
CRINKLE CRAGS
HARTER FELL
GREAT CARRS
SWIRL HOW
WETHERLAM
BRIM FELL
WANSFELL PIKE
TROUTBECK TONGUE
SOUR HOWES
CONISTON OLD MAN
S

MILES 1 2 3 4 5 6 7 8 9 10 11 12 13 14 15 16 17

Lakes and Tarns

SSW: *Windermere* (two sections)
NNW: The upper reach of *Ullswater* may be seen by descending the west slope for 50 yards, or by following the wall north. **N**: *Hayeswater* is brought into view by a short walk (130 yards) in the direction of High Street.

THE VIEW

The tall column, the wall, and adjacent high ground northwards between them interrupt the panorama — and various 'stations' must be visited to see all there is to see. The view is good, but not amongst the best; the northern prospect, in particular, is best surveyed from the slope going down to Threshthwaite Mouth.

The best feature in the scene is Windermere, to which the Troutbeck valley leads the eye with excellent effect.

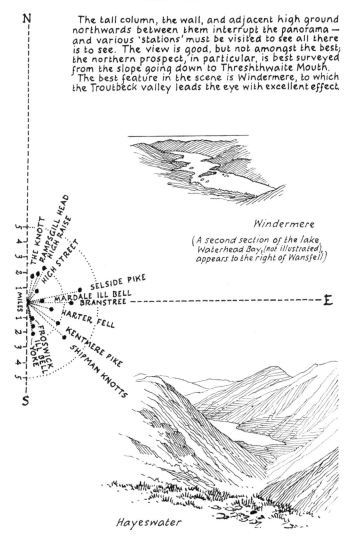

Windermere

(A second section of the lake, Waterhead Bay, (not illustrated) appears to the right of Wansfell)

Hayeswater

RIDGE ROUTES

To CAUDALE MOOR, 2502' : 1 mile : NW, W and WSW
Depression at 1950' : 560 feet of ascent
A rough scramble, made safe in mist by walls

There is more to this walk than appears at first sight, for the gap of Threshthwaite Mouth is deep and it links slopes that are steep and rough. Keep by the wall until the broken crag of Caudale is left behind. The Caudale flank above the gap can be dangerous when the rocks are iced or under snow.

To GRAY CRAG, 2286' : 1¼ miles : slightly W of N
Two minor depressions : 150 feet of ascent
An easy, interesting walk, better avoided in mist.

Straightforward walking along the descending and narrowing north ridge leads first to the nameless conical height of point 2331', then to the flat top of Gray Crag. Two broken walls are crossed en route. Both flanks are heavily scarped and dangerous in mist.

To FROSWICK, 2359'
1 mile
SSE then S and SE
Depression at 2100'
300 feet of ascent
A very easy walk

Follow the wall SSE, slanting along the line of the old fence to a stout straining-post, where the path along the ridge may be joined. A long grassy descent leads to the final rise to the top of Froswick

RIDGE ROUTES

To HIGH STREET, 2718′ : 1¼ miles : SE, then E and NE
Depression at 2475′ : 250 feet of ascent
A very simple walk, safe in mist
Follow the wall to its eastern terminus, avoid the bog there, and continue along the line of an old fence to join another wall that runs directly to and beyond the top of High Street. All is grass.

To MARDALE ILL BELL, 2496′
1⅓ miles : SE, then E, ENE and ESE
Depressions at 2475′ and 2350′ : 200 feet of ascent
Easy walking, but a confusing area in mist
Leave the corner of the High Street wall by a plain track trending eastwards and when this becomes indistinct keep on over long grass in the same direction, descending slightly to the depression ahead. In mist, take care not to descend to the right into Hall Cove.

*Thornthwaite Crag
from the south ridge of
Caudale Moor*

Troutbeck Tongue

properly named
The Tongue, Troutbeck Park

from the Kirkstone-Windermere road

CAUDALE MOOR

▲ ILL BELL

TROUTBECK
TONGUE

● Troutbeck

MILES

0   1   2   3

There are many Tongues in Lakeland, all of them wedges of high or rising ground between enclosing becks that join below at the tip, but none is more distinctive or aptly named than that in the middle of the Troutbeck Valley. Other Tongues usually have their roots high on a mountainside, but this one thrusts forward from the floor of the dalehead. Although of very modest altitude, it has an attraction for the gentler pedestrian as a viewpoint for the valley, and makes an admirable short excursion in pleasant scenery from Windermere or Troutbeck or, by Skelghyll Woods, from Ambleside.

MAP

A small solitary tree helps to locate the old cairn on the brow of the hill. The hoary stones now serve as a double shelter.

N

ONE MILE

continuation CAUDALE MOOR 3

continuation FROSWICK 2

continuation CAUDALE MOOR 3

Trout Beck

old cairn

continuation ILL BELL 3

continuation YOKE 3

TROUTBECK TONGUE ▲ 1191

quarry

gates

Trout Beck

Troutbeck Park Farm →

Hagg Bridge

gate

TROUTBECK 1½

WINDERMERE 5

ASCENTS

A prominent rock rib descends southwards from the summit and indicates the quickest and pleasantest route to the top; if desired the rocks can be easily avoided. The longer way, along the Tongue from its northern root is the simplest of walks (visit the ancient cairn) but the pattern of the irrigation ditches here is a warning to expect much marshy ground.

THE SUMMIT

CAUDALE MOOR   GRAY CRAG over Threshthwaite Mouth   THORNTHWAITE CRAG

The rocky scramble up the south ridge from the cart-track is entertaining enough to hold out the promise of a summit equally interesting, but the promise is not fulfilled by the reality, which is a grassy knoll a little higher than several more nearby, and graced by a small heap of stones. Apart from the view down the valley to Windermere, nothing here is worth comment.

Slate bridge, Trout Beck

THE VIEW

Troutbeck Tongue is set deep in the bottom of a great bowl of hills, all of which overtop it and limit the scene. Only to the south is there an open view — of Windermere — but there is also a peep of distant fells to the west.

Principal Fells

N

Hart Crag (Caudale Moor)

CAUDALE MOOR

RED SCREES

GRAY CRAG

THORNTHWAITE CRAG

FROSWICK

ILL BELL

YOKE

SCAFELL PIKE

W — — — — — — E

BOWFELL

CRINKLE CRAGS

PIKE O' BLISCO

5 miles

2½ miles

10 miles

WANSFELL

Dodd Hill (Wansfell)

SALLOWS

SOUR HOWES

S

Lakes and Tarns

SSW : *Windermere*
(middle and lower reaches)

Windermere and the Troutbeck Valley

Wansfell

CAUDALE ▲ MOOR

▲ RED SCREES

▲ WANSFELL
● Ambleside

● Troutbeck

MILES
0   1   2   3

from High Grove

NATURAL FEATURES

Caudale Moor sends out three distinct ridges to the south, and the most westerly and longest of the three descends to a wide depression (crossed by the Kirkstone road) before rising and narrowing along an undulating spur that finally falls to the shores of Windermere. This spur is Wansfell, and, although its summit-ridge is fairly narrow and well-defined, the slopes on most sides are extensive, the fell as a whole occupying a broad tract of territory between Ambleside and the Troutbeck valley. Except northwards, the lower slopes are attractively wooded; the upper reaches are mainly grassy, but at the south-west extremity of the ridge there is a rocky bluff known as Wansfell Pike, which is commonly but incorrectly regarded as the top of the fell. Other crags, masked by trees, flank the Kirkstone road at Troutbeck and Jenkins Crag in Skelghyll Woods is a very popular viewpoint. The main streams flow from marshy ground east of the ridge — this was the scene of the cloudburst in June 1953 and these the gentle becks that suddenly became raging torrents and caused so much damage in the Troutbeck district.

MAP

MAP

N

continuation
WANSFELL 2

Salutation Hotel

Stock Ghyll

Middle
Grove

footbridge

WANSFELL
1597

Stock Ghyll
Force

stile

gate

school

Ambleside

ruin

gasworks

Blue Hill Road
Old Lake Road

gate

Wansfell
Pike 1581

culvert

gate
and stile

tower

old quarry

gate

Skelghyll
Wood

gates

Cascades

aqueduct
observatory

Romney
Hotel

Kelsick
Scar

Jenkins
Crag

High
Skelghyll

ruin

old
quarry

WINDERMERE

continuation on opposite page

Windermere

ONE MILE

MAP

continuation
WANSFELL 2

An old path (Low Kingate) enables the walker from Troutbeck to Kirkstone to avoid a mile of the hard main road — a consideration in summer.

Kirkstone-Windermere Road

Low Kingate

The Troutbeck Valley

1200 · 1300 · 1300 · 1200 · 1100 · 1000

1400

Dodd Hill

1500

old quarry

WANSFELL 1597'

Raven Crag

1500 · 1400

Chimney Crag

culvert

1300 · 1200 · 1100 · 1000

Stony Beck

800

gate and stile

700 · 600

gate

500

Town Head

Scot Bridge

Queen's Head Hotel

Nanny Lane

Mortal Man Hotel

St Margarets Well

1000

WINDERMERE 3½

Troutbeck

N

Institute

900 · 800 · 700

ONE MILE

continuation on opposite page

Town End

AMBLESIDE 3¾

WINDERMERE 3

ASCENT FROM AMBLESIDE
1500 feet of ascent : 2½ miles

WANSFELL

Wansfell Pike

Wansfell Pike is in sight throughout the climb from Stock Ghyll; the slope steepens as height is gained. This is a pleasant approach, but the ridge is less attractive.

MIDDLE GROVE ¾ ⟵

The approach by the lane behind the gasworks is NOT recommended, for reasons palpable to all who venture there.

Stock Ghyll

Stock Ghyll Force

ruin

stiles

gate

school

Blue Hill Road

gasworks

looking east-south-east

Ambleside

ASCENT FROM TROUTBECK
1100 feet of ascent : 1¾ miles

Wansfell Pike

WANSFELL

Dodd Hill

route indicated by stakes

culvert

gate and Stile

The Troutbeck side of the fell is rather dreary; the advantage of this approach is the sudden revelation of the view when the ridge is gained.

After rain, Nanny Lane is hardly better than a river-bed (complete with river) in its lower part.

Nanny Lane starts 90 yards north of St. Margaret's Well.

If both summits are visited, it is advisable to ascend Wansfell first — the best views will then be in front on the traverse to Wansfell Pike.

Dodd Hill is the finest viewpoint for the Troutbeck valley, but cannot be reached without climbing a wall.

Nanny Lane

KIRKSTONE ⟶

looking north-west

St. Margaret's Well ⟶

Mortal Man Hotel

Troutbeck

THE SUMMIT

CAUDALE MOOR   THORNTHWAITE CRAG

Kirkstone Pass

Threshthwaite Mouth

A grassy hummock, a little higher than many around, is the true summit of the fell: a few small stones confirm it. It is an unattractive place, rarely visited; better is the rocky top of Wansfell Pike, which at least is mildly interesting and unique in possessing an iron gate. The higher summit lies 150 yards east of the ridge-wall, which, in mist, is a safe guide as far as Wansfell Pike, whence paths go down to Ambleside (west) and Troutbeck (east).

The view westwards from Jenkins Crag

1 : Coniston Old Man
2 : Brim Fell
3 : Wetherlam
4 : Wrynose Pass
5 : Cold Pike
6 : Pike o'Blisco
7 : Crinkle Crags
8 : Scafell
9 : Bowfell
10 : Esk Pike
11 : Great End
12 : Loft Crag
13 : Pike o'Stickle
14 : Harrison Stickle
15 : Pavey Ark
16 : Little Langdale
17 : Great Langdale
18 : Black Fell
19 : Park Fell
20 : Lingmoor Fell
21 : Loughrigg Fell

THE VIEW
FROM THE SUMMIT OF WANSFELL

As a viewpoint, the highest part of the summit is inferior to the lower Wansfell Pike, and, curiously, fewer fells can be seen. Nevertheless, the prospect westwards is very charming.

Principal Fells

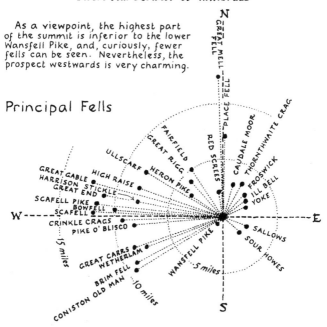

Lakes and Tarns

S : Windermere
WSW : Little Langdale Tarn
W : Grasmere
W : Rydal Water

Red Screes, from the summit

THE VIEW
FROM WANSFELL PIKE

Wansfell Pike excels in its view of Windermere, the graceful curve of the lake showing to great advantage. Westwards, the scene is especially beautiful. Red Screes is a fine object in the north; the east is dull.

Principal Fells

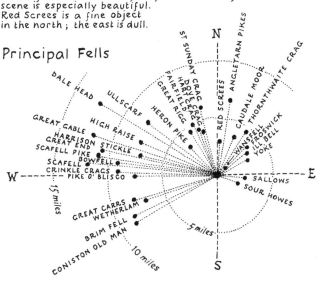

Lakes and Tarns

S : *Windermere*
SW : *Bletham Tarn*
W : *Little Langdale Tarn*
WNW : *Grasmere*
WNW : *Rydal Water*
The two sheets of water on the lower slopes of Sour Howes, southeast, are reservoirs.

Windermere, from Wansfell Pike

RIDGE ROUTE

To CAUDALE MOOR, 2502'
4½ miles : N, then NE and E
Depression at 1100'
1550 feet of ascent
A long, easy, uninteresting trudge.

Although this is the natural high-level approach to the High Street range from Ambleside, it is not a regular walkers' route in the section between Wansfell and St. Raven's Edge, and awkward walls have to be climbed that were not built to be climbed. On grass all the way. Safe in mist, but marshy patches will then prove unpleasant.

Aqueduct Observatory above Kelsick Scar

There are two such edifices, and a tower, above the line of the Thirlmere aqueduct along the southern slopes of Wansfell Pike.

Locating them is a pleasant way of spending a halfday: an art lies in doing this *sans* wallscaling.

Stock Ghyll Force

Wether Hill

2210'
approx

spelt 'Weather' Hill
on Bartholomew's map

from Beda Fell

Howtown

LOADPOT
▲ HILL

Bampton

▲
WETHER HILL

▲ HIGH RAISE

MILES

0 1 2 3 4

NATURAL FEATURES

The High Street range has largely lost its appeal to the walker by the time he reaches the twin grassy mounds of Wether Hill on the long tramp along its spine northwards, and there is nothing here to call for a halt. The top, scarcely higher than the general level of the ridge, is quite without interest, while the eastern slopes are little better although traversed by two good routes from Bampton; but the western flank, characteristically steeper, has the peculiarity of Gowk Hill, a subsidiary height which itself develops into a parallel ridge running north: this encloses, with the main ridge, the little hidden valley of Fusedale. The best features of Wether Hill, paradoxically, are found in its valleys: eastwards, Cawdale Beck and Measand Beck have attractions rarely visited except by the lone shepherd; westwards, Fusedale Beck is fed from two wooded ravines, and here too is lovely Martindale.

looking south

1 : The summit
2 : Ridge continuing to High Raise
3 : Ridge continuing to Loadpot Hill
4 : High Kop
5 : Low Kop
6 : Gowk Hill
7 : Steel Knotts
8 : River Lowther
9 : Haweswater Beck
10 : Cawdale Beck
11 : Willdale Beck
12 : Fusedale Beck
13 : Howe Grain
14 : Martindale
15 : Ullswater

BRANSTREE   HARTER FELL   MARDALE ILL BELL
  Gatesgarth   Nan Bield
    Pass   Pass

Haweswater
from the Standing Stones above Burn Banks

MAP

Wether Hill's slopes sprawl extensively
eastwards, descending gradually in easy
ridges to a wide belt of cultivated land
west of the Bampton - Burn Banks road—
from which the ascent will generally be
commenced on this side. No details of
this cultivated area are depicted on the
following maps (on pages 5 and 6) other
than those necessary to get the walker to
the open fell as quickly as possible.

MAP

The eastern slopes of Wether Hill are bounded on the north by Cawdale Beck and on the south by Measand Beck, but some detail of the adjacent fells is, in addition, given below because they carry routes that lead onto Wether Hill.

N

ONE MILE

continuation
LOADPOT HILL 4

continuation LOADPOT HILL 5

continuation opposite

continuation overleaf

continuation HIGH RAISE 4

Cawdale Beck

Cawdale

The Hause

White Bog

old quarry

sheepfold

hut

ruin

Seathole Grain

Atkinson's Grain

Low Kop

groove

ruin
(old quarry)

tarns

Measand Beck

sheepfold

groove

ruin

waterfall

Measand End

groove

Lad Crags

ruin

rain gauge

MAP

ONE MILE

NOTE:
Within these enclosing walls, almost all is cultivated farmland, of little interest to walkers bound for high places. No details of this area are given.

see NOTE below

ROAD TO HAWESWATER HOTEL AND MARDALE HEAD

MAP

HELTON 2½

Bampton

quarry

gate

Hall

fall

SHAP 4

school

400

700

see note on opposite page

continuation opposite

700

Burn Banks

HAWESWATER HOTEL AND MARDALE HEAD

N

ONE MILE

The stake on Hause End

Slate bridge, Cawdale Beck

Waterfalls, Hows Beck

ASCENTS FROM HOWTOWN AND MARTINDALE
1750 feet of ascent, 3 miles, from Howtown
1550 feet of ascent, 2½ miles, from Martindale old church

The ruined hut by the wall is a prominent object on the final stages of the climb and is the point to aim for when descending

Steel Knotts, from Fusedale

A first-class variation, especially in descending to Howtown, is to follow the ridge of Steel Knotts — but NOT in mist

looking south

There are many fells more worthy of climbing than Wether Hill, the final slope being very dull, but there are no more delightful starting-points than Howtown and Martindale, the approach from the latter being especially good — until the last slope is reached.

ASCENTS FROM BURN BANKS AND BAMPTON
1550 feet of ascent from Burn Banks; 1750 from Bampton.
4½ miles from Burn Banks direct, 5 via Measand Beck;
5 miles from Bampton

At the bifurcation of paths in the
Burn Banks plantation, keep right.

The Bampton route *via* Hause End is easy
and interesting; the Burn Banks route across the open
common is a little confusing in its early stages; on a hot
day the Measand route, although pathless, is attractive.

THE SUMMIT

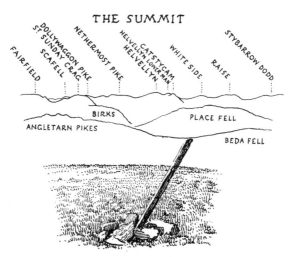

FAIRFIELD · SCAFELL · DOLLYWAGGON PIKE · ST SUNDAY CRAG · NETHERMOST PIKE · HELVELLYN LOWER MAN · HELVELLYN · CATSTYCAM · WHITE SIDE · RAISE · STYBARROW DODD

ANGLETARN PIKES · BIRKS · PLACE FELL · BEDA FELL

Two rounded grassy mounds of similar altitude, separated by a slight depression, form the summit. The more extensive of the two mounds, the southern, is quite featureless: the small northern mound is the recognised top and carries a wooden stake set in a small cairn (one stone of which is a boundary stone lying on its side). The summit is popular with grazing animals of various species, but humans will find it a dreary and uninteresting place. The High Street crosses the top, but along here is barely noticeable, being no more distinct than a sheep-trod.

DESCENTS: All slopes are easy, and it is a waste of time to look for the few paths. For Bampton, pass over High Kop to join one of two good grooves. For Martindale and Howtown descend west to the ruin by the prominent broken crosswall below: leave the ruin on the *right*, passing through the gateway in the wall, for Martindale; but for Fusedale and Howtown leave the ruin well to the left.

In mist, there is little danger of accident, but keep out of stream-beds which run in ravines.

The boundary stone, High Kop, with High Raise in the background

THE VIEW

Principal Fells

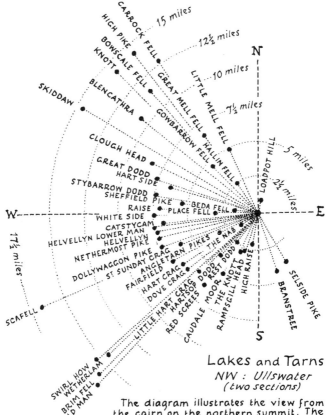

Lakes and Tarns
NW : Ullswater
(two sections)

The diagram illustrates the view from the cairn on the northern summit. The view from the southern summit is the same substantially, but in addition Scafell Pike can be seen. There is a wide prospect of the Pennines, but undoubtedly the best feature is the finely-grouped Helvellyn and Fairfield fells across the rough, romantic Martindale country.

RIDGE ROUTES

To LOADPOT HILL, 2201' : 1 mile : N
Depression at 2025' : 180 feet of ascent

An easy walk, safe in mist
Keep to the left side of the
depression (a faint track
materialises) to avoid the
peat-hags that cut deeply
into the old path (the High
Street) on the right side.
Make a beeline for the
chimney-stack ahead —
the summit (quartz cairn)
is directly beyond.

To HIGH RAISE, 2634'
*2¼ miles : SSW
Depression at 2150'
500 feet of ascent*

A long, easy walk, safe in mist.
Cross both summits to the
depression south (peat-hags
and stony ravines here have
carved away the High Street)
and ascend a distinct groove
to the wall-corner ahead. The route follows the wall south: it may
be crossed near Redcrag Tarn for the best views, but on a gusty
day it offers shelter if kept immediately on the right. When the
wall ends at a short fence, above a steep ravine, the path climbs
across the open fell. The cairn is among stones 100 yards away
to the left of the path at its highest point.

Measand Beck

The Forces of Measand Beck, near its outlet into Haweswater, need no introduction to frequenters of this area, but the waterfalls illustrated, two miles upstream, are rarely seen.

Yoke

2309'

spelt 'Yolk' on some Ordnance Survey maps

▲ HIGH STREET

▲ ILL BELL

▲ YOKE

● Kentmere

● Troutbeck

MILES
0 1 2 3 4

from the Kirkstone-Windermere road

NATURAL FEATURES

Yoke is best known as the southern outpost of the Ill Bell ridge leading up to High Street from Garburn Pass, and is usually dismissed as a dull unattractive mound. As seen from Troutbeck, this seems a quite accurate assessment, but the Kentmere flank is very different, abounding in interest. On this side, below the summit, is the formidable thousand-foot precipice of Rainsborrow Crag (the safety of which is a subject of disagreement between rock-climbers and foxes) and, rising above Kentmere village, is a knobbly spur that looks like the knuckles of a clenched fist—a place of rocky excrescences, craggy tors and tumbled boulders, and a fine playground for the mountaineering novice. Both flanks of Yoke carry the scars of old quarrying operations.

grass

12

bracken

17

2

bracken

16

11

15

1 : The summit
2 : Garburn Pass
3 : Rainsborrow Crag
4 : Skeel Crags
5 : Buck Crag
6 : Castle Crag
7 : Piked Howes
8 : Ewe Crags
9 : Cowsty Knotts
10 : Raven Crag
11 : Badger Rock
12 : Lowther Brow
13 : Kentmere Reservoir
14 : Bryant's Gill
15 : River Kent
16 : Hall Gill
17 : Trout Beck

looking north

Yoke 3

MAP

continuation ILL BELL 3

Star Crag

old quarry

N

ONE MILE

TROUTBECK TONGUE

gate

cart-track

Flagg Gill

gates

YOKE 2309'

falls

Park Quarry

gates

gap

stile

continuation opposite

gate

gates

TROUTBECK 2

Lowther Brow

old quarry

gate Den

Trout Beck

sheepfold

Green Grove Gill

Ing Bridge

grid

gate

Miles Gill

gate

Long Green Head

cart-track

Garburn Pass

Troutbeck Valley

Garburn Road

SALLOWS

continuation
SOUR HOWES 2

MAP

Kentmere Reservoir

continuation ILL BELL 3

dam

continuation HARTER FELL

quarry

Rainsborrow Cove

Kentmere Valley

River Kent

quarries

Star Crag

YOKE 2309

Rainsborrow Crag

Skeel Crags

gate

gate

Briars Gill

cart track

Hartrigg

gate

gap and stile

fold

continuation opposite

gate sheep-pen

Hart Crag

Scale Knotts

Saletarn Knotts

Rowantree Knott

Birk Rigg

Scales

gate

gap

Castle Crag

Piked Howes

Raven Crag

gates

Buck Crag

Ewe Crags

Kentmere

gate

Brow Top

sheepfold

ruin x

Hall Gill

gate

Badger Rock

gates

gate

Church

Kentmere Hall

Garburn Pass

gate

gate

Low Bridge

SALLOWS

STAVELEY 4

ONE MILE

N

ASCENT FROM GARBURN PASS
850 feet of ascent : 1¾ miles

YOKE

path to
ILL BELL

2300

2200

2100

2000

stile
and gap

tarn

1900

1800

1700

Upper
Kentmere
Valley

Troutbeck
Valley

Above the wall
there is no path
for 100 yards but
one will be found
higher up the slope

Rainsborrow
Crag

old
quarry

tarn

quarry path

1600

gate
sheep pen

Lowther Brow

25 yards beyond the stream
a big cairn indicates the
indistinct turn to the
right from the main
path to the quarry.

Buck
Crag

Leave the pass at the point
where it turns sharply. The
first few yards are abominably
marshy. Aim for the small
cairns ahead.

1500

The variation start
from the pass, by the
wall, is very marshy

gate

KENTMERE
1¼

gate

Garburn
Pass
1475'
(spelt Garbourn Pass
on Ordnance Survey maps)

looking north

TROUTBECK 2
WINDERMERE 4½

1400

The easy slopes of Lowther Brow seem to offer an
alternative route from Troutbeck, but the promising tracks
climbing through the bracken from the cart-road behind Long Green
Head (see map) do not continue far and the ascent becomes tiresome.
The route depicted here, from Garburn Pass, is better in every way.

This is a dull, easy walk, but the dreary foreground
is relieved by the splendid views to the west. There
are patches of marshy ground to the 1800' contour —
the route throughout is on grass.

ASCENT FROM KENTMERE
1800 feet of ascent : 2½ miles (3 miles via Garburn Pass)

Badger Rock (or Brock Stone) has many rock-climbs of all degrees of difficulty.

looking north-west

Several tracks lead up the fell from the valley-lanes, apparently bound for Yoke, but only the path to Garburn Pass continues as far as the ridge.

Although Garburn Pass offers the easiest route, the craggy screen rising steeply behind the village will tempt the more adventurous walker: the top of the spur is a maze worth exploring, but only the route depicted guarantees to avoid unclimbable walls.

THE SUMMIT

ILL BELL
HIGH STREET
MARDALE ILL BELL

The highest point on the broad grassy top is a small rock-sided platform with a cairn. A wire fence forms a right-angle nearby. Another cairn (a better viewpoint) stands 130 yards to the south.

DESCENTS: A short descent down the western slope brings into view a good track skirting the summit: this, followed to the left (south) leads to the wall that goes down to Garburn Pass.

In mist, note that the north-east and east slopes are entirely dangerous, and that the lower western flank is very rough: it features, in a walled enclosure, the bracken-concealed, fearful abyss of Park Quarry, a fall into which would definitely end the day's walk. From the top cairn, descend west (170 yards only) to the track; or, if uncertain of the compass points, follow the wire fence left, and left again at another angle — the track will be picked up as it crosses the fence at a broken stile. Turn left (south) along the track, which becomes indistinct but points the direction of the wall going down to Garburn Pass.

ILL BELL
scree gully
Star Crag
broken stile
grass
best view of Kentmere Reservoir
2200
grass
direction of → RAINSBORROW CRAG
△ best view of Windermere
grass
2200
GARBURN PASS
YARDS
0   100   200

Park Quarry — in the sheltered depths of which flowers bloom and ferns flourish in December

THE VIEW

This is a good viewpoint, more particularly for the wide sweep of country and sea southwards. Of the Lakeland scene, the prospect due west is especially attractive.

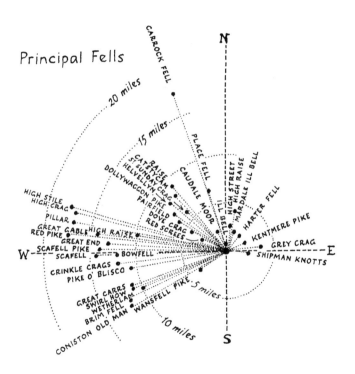

Principal Fells

Lakes and Tarns

SSW : *Windermere* (*much better seen from the south cairn : a very beautiful view*)

SW : *Blelham Tarn*

—————— *To see Kentmere Reservoir, visit the edge of Star Crag, where the reservoir comes suddenly and dramatically into view north-east*

RIDGE ROUTE

To ILL BELL, 2476' : ⅔ mile : N
Depression at 2180' : 300 feet of ascent
An easy climb, safe in mist

Cross the fence and proceed down to and
across the depression with the escarpment
close by on the right. This is a simple walk
in clear weather, but, although there is no
difficulty in mist, it may then be not quite
easy to get safely off the top of Ill Bell.

HALF A MILE

Raven Crag

Buck Crag

Badger Rock
(Brock Stone)

West face

East face

This isolated rock stands within fifty yards of the Garburn path, just
beyond the last buildings of Kentmere. A well-known local landmark,
it has little fame outside the valley. Although the base of the rock
is now silted up, there is little doubt that it is a boulder fallen from
the fellside above, a theory supported by the cavities beneath (a
refuge for foxes), and it may well be the biggest boulder in Lakeland.
There are rock-climbs on it of all degrees of difficulty.

Rainsborrow Crag

THE FAR EASTERN FELLS
Some Personal Notes
in conclusion

It would be very remiss of me if I did not take this first opportunity publicly to acknowledge, with sincere gratitude, the many kind and encouraging letters that followed the publication of Book One. There have also been offers of hospitality, of transport (I have no car nor any wish for one), of company and of collaboration, and of financial help — all of which I have declined as gracefully as I could whilst feeling deeply appreciative, for I am stubbornly resolved that this must be a single-handed effort. I have set myself this task, and I am pigheaded enough to want to do it without help. So far, everything is all right. Sufficient copies of Book One were sold to pay the printer's bill, and here again I must thank all readers who recommended the book to others, for it is perfectly clear that, lacking full facilities for publicity and distribution, it could hardly have succeeded otherwise.

I have just completed the last page of Book Two, and feel like a man who has come home from a long and lonely journey. Rarely did I meet anyone on my explorations of the High Street fells. Usually I walked from morning till dusk without a sight of human beings. This is the way I like it, but what joys have been mine that other folk should share! Let me make a plea for the exhilarating hills that form the subject of this book. They should not remain neglected. To walk upon them, to tramp the ridges, to look from their tops across miles of glorious country, is constant delight. But the miles are long, and from one place of accommodation to another they are many. The Far Eastern Fells are for the strong walker and should please the solitary man of keen observation and imagination. Animal and bird life is much in evidence, and not the least of the especial charms of the area is the frequent sight of herds of ponies and deer that make these wild heights their home.

Perhaps I have been a little unkind to Manchester Corporation in referring to Mardale and Swindale in this book. If we can accept as absolutely necessary the conversion of Haweswater, then it must be conceded that Manchester have done the job as unobtrusively as possible. Mardale is still a noble valley. But man works with such clumsy hands! Gone for ever are the quiet wooded bays and shingly shores that nature had fashioned so sweetly in the Haweswater of old; how aggressively ugly is the tidemark of the new Haweswater! A cardinal mistake has been made, from the walker's point of view, in choosing the site for the new hotel: much more convenient would have been a re-built Dun Bull at the head of the valley, or better still amongst the trees of The Rigg. For a walker who can call upon transport, however, the new road gives splendid access to the heart of the fells.

I leave this area to renew acquaintance with the more popular and frequented heights in the middle of Lakeland — the Langdale, Grasmere and Keswick triangle. This is a beautiful part of the district, and I shall enjoy it; but it is a weakness of mine to be for ever looking back, and often I shall reflect on the haunting loneliness of High Street and the supreme loveliness of Ullswater. It will please me then to think that this book may perhaps help to introduce to others the quiet delights that have been mine during the past two years.

Autumn, 1956   AW.